Beethoven's Piano Music

Unlocking the Masters Series, No. 23

Series Editor: Robert Levine

Beethoven's Piano Music

A Listener's Guide

Victor Lederer

AMADEUS
PRESS

An Imprint of Hal Leonard Corporation

Published in 2011 by Amadeus Press
An Imprint of Hal Leonard Corporation
7777 West Bluemound Road
Milwaukee, WI 53213

Trade Book Division Editorial Offices
33 Plymouth St., Montclair, NJ 07042

Printed in the United States of America

Book design by Snow Creative Services

Library of Congress Cataloging-in-Publication Data

Lederer, Victor.
    Beethoven's piano music : a listener's guide / Victor Lederer. — 1st pbk. ed.
        p. cm. — (Unlocking the masters series ; no. 23)
    Includes bibliographical references.
    ISBN 978-1-57467-194-0
    1. Beethoven, Ludwig van, 1770-1827. Piano music. 2. Beethoven, Ludwig van, 1770-1827. Concertos, piano, orchestra. 3. Piano music—19th century—History and criticism. I. Title.
    ML410.B4L293 2011
    786.2092—dc22
                                                                        2011000282

www.amadeuspress.com

For Bernard Rose, my teacher and friend

Contents

Acknowledgments   ix

Chapter 1. Beethoven and the Piano   1

Chapter 2. Some Aspects of Beethoven's Life   13

Chapter 3. The First, Second, and Third Concertos: 23
    Under Mozart's Influence

Chapter 4. The Fourth and Fifth Concertos   35

Chapter 5. The Earliest Sonatas: Opp. 2, 7, 10, and 13,   47
    the "Pathétique"

Chapter 6. Early-Middle Masterworks: Sonatas 9–15   61

Chapter 7. The High Middle Period: Sonatas 16–23   73

Chapter 8. Five Transitional Sonatas   91

Chapter 9. The "Hammerklavier" Sonata   105

Chapter 10. The Final Trilogy   117

Chapter 11. The Bagatelles and Other Short Pieces   133

Chapter 12. The Variations   143

Chapter 13. Beethoven the Companion   153

Notes   157

Selected Bibliography   161

CD Track Listing   163

Acknowledgments

Thanks are due for this book to a larger number of my friends and extended family than it's sensible to list, but they know who they are. Thanks to my editor and dear friend Bob Levine. All my love and gratitude, as always, to Elaine, Paul, and Karen.

Beethoven and the Piano

Some of Beethoven's music for piano is so well known and frequently heard, so common to the experience of anyone who can claim basic musical literacy, that to cite his crucial role as a composer for the instrument seems almost silly. Among Beethoven's sonatas, the "Pathétique," the "Moonlight," the "Waldstein," and the "Appassionata" stand alongside Shakespeare's best-loved plays and the art of Michelangelo as unassailable coin of the (Western) cultural realm. And the popularity of his five concertos for piano and orchestra, particularly the Fifth, nicknamed the "Emperor," continues unabated among audiences, who never seem to tire of them, in recordings or in live performance.

When planning recital programs, pianists come back again and again to Beethoven and Chopin as the two most important composers for their instrument, whose music appeals most to the public and best demonstrates the performer's technique and artistry. Chopin's music, conceived with an uncanny feel for the nature and capabilities of the piano, seems to leap from the instrument's throat—as if it actually had one—like that of his friend Bellini's for the voice. Of course Beethoven knew the instrument well too, but the integrity of an idea sometimes dominated his sense of sound even before he went deaf, and as a result the music can be clumsy in its layout on the keyboard, as Chopin's never is. We readily forgive Beethoven his occasional awkwardness for the sake of his sublimity. In any case, these two giants form the very heart of the pianist's repertory.

They are surrounded, not followed, by Bach and Debussy. Bach composed for earlier instruments, the clavichord and harpsichord, but pianists have adopted his works for their obvious power, energy, and spiritual grandeur. Debussy, the giant of early modernism, composed a relatively small oeuvre of utterly idiomatic music for the piano that gloriously spans the gulf between the romantic and modern eras; it grows in esteem and influence and turns up with ever-greater frequency in recital as the decades pass. Schumann and Schubert stand close behind, thanks to a few crucial pieces each. Schumann's case is particularly striking: pianists and audiences could never live without his bare dozen of early masterpieces, but apart from these, little else is performed or, apparently, wanted by the public. Similarly, Schubert is known for six or eight great sonatas, the eight peerless impromptus, the *Moments musicaux*, and a few isolated pieces. The *Wanderer Fantasy*, a flawed, sonata-like work on a large scale, used to be popular but seems to be losing ground.

Most of Mozart's sonatas are magnificent, as are the individual works such as the Rondo in A Minor, K. 511, and the Adagio in B Minor, K. 540; but few pianists seem willing to play more than one in a recital program. And Haydn's wonderful keyboard works—highly inventive sonatas, for the most part—seem doomed to the same fate. Everyone loves and respects them, but one seems to go a long way in the course of an evening's music making. But offer an all-Beethoven or an all-Chopin recital, and no one complains.

Beethoven's popularity is easy to explain: his music is beautiful, powerful, and deep. We may feel challenged by it, but we are stirred, too, and the composer's very human voice can be heard clearly through its formidable technical complexities. This is why yet another book about Beethoven may be useful for those who admire his music and want better to understand how it works and why it is so intellectually and emotionally effective, but who feel intimidated by the obvious technical challenges it poses.

Like Mozart and Chopin, Beethoven was a pianist-composer: the piano was the instrument he played, composed at, and performed on in public. Like Mozart, Beethoven was a child prodigy on the instrument, a gift his abusive father hoped to cash in on. His career as a composer for the instrument began early and ran almost to the end of his life. Beethoven's second set of published works, his Opus 2, consisted of the three piano sonatas covered in chapter 5, and his last were the six short Bagatelles Op. 126 of 1824 (see chapter 11 for a look at these mostly tiny masterworks). In between, he composed thirty-two sonatas that form the bulk of his output for solo piano, including the famous ones mentioned above, as well as some that are surprisingly little-known except by professional musicians. Which, as we also shall see, is a shame. Others, like Op. 101 and the "Hammerklavier," Op. 106, are well-known, and feared for the formidable challenges they pose to the technique of the player and the intellectual focus of player and listener alike. The final three sonatas, Opp. 109, 110, and 111, are sublime works of the composer's late maturity.

Chapters 5 through 10 are devoted to that core of the piano repertory, the thirty-two sonatas, which Beethoven composed over nearly three decades of his creative life. They display an extraordinary development from the first to the last. Even in the earliest, which demonstrate his respect for Haydn and Mozart, Beethoven already speaks his own unmistakable musical language. Several of the early sonatas show some structural similarities, but their contents are never alike. And beginning with No. 12, in A-flat Major, Op. 26, composed in 1800, they are all singular in form, as well. The closest parallel in music to this beautiful arc might be the operas of Verdi, which show that master's fierce determination not to repeat himself and to reveal fresh musical and, in Verdi's case, dramatic concepts in each new work. A couple of Beethoven's sonatas—say, Op. 22 and Op. 31 No. 1—are backward-looking, just as *Il trovatore* and *Aida* might be considered Verdi's operas of consolidation. But the two composers are equally purposeful in developing and refining their styles.

Chapter 11 will cover the short but worthwhile bagatelles, mentioned above, which come in three sets: Op. 33 (1802), then Op. 119 (1820–22), and Op. 126 (1824). Finally, Beethoven composed many sets of variations for solo piano. Four or five are significant; one, the *Thirty-three Variations on a Waltz by Diabelli*, Op. 120, completed in 1823, is Beethoven's last major work for solo piano and, to some, the pinnacle not only of the master's piano works, but of all compositions in variation form. We'll take a look at these in chapter 12.

Beethoven composed five concertos for piano and orchestra, the first three as vehicles for his own performances, as was typical for pianist-composers of the day. In a quirk of publication order, the concerto numbered second was composed first, and thus the delicious Concerto No. 2, Op. 19, has its feet firmly planted in the eighteenth century. After this work, each grows bigger and bolder, culminating in the sublime No. 4, Op. 58, of 1805–6, and No. 5—the titanic yet tranquil "Emperor" Concerto, Op. 73, of 1809. All are heard often, with the last two maintaining immense popularity. These concertos are of course as important within their genre as they can be, and in fact few have followed of comparable aesthetic stature. But Beethoven himself would probably not claim that he advanced the expressive possibilities of the form beyond what Mozart accomplished, larger in scale though his compositions are. We'll look at these magnificent works in chapters 3 and 4.

Beethoven started his career as a virtuoso pianist and composer, playing in the salons of wealthy patrons, usually aristocrats, as well as in public concerts, which were different in form from what we are familiar with today. He might play a solo, then accompany a singer, then improvise a "fantasy" on a theme requested by his patron, usually an operatic or popular melody. Beethoven's mastery of the piano is clear from the technical difficulty of nearly everything he composed for the instrument: with the exception of the popular little bagatelle "Für Elise," it's all hard to play, and in some cases—the "Waldstein," "Hammerklavier," and Op. 101 sonatas—for master pianists only. But the piano was the instrument and the piano sonata the primary venue he returned to again and again as the proving ground for new ideas, just as he did with almost every form he used.

Beethoven's own playing was a source of wonderment to those who heard him. He was by all accounts one of the most brilliant pianists of his age. From his youth, the excellence of his improvisations—at that time an important demonstration of a pianist's skill—was remarked on. Listeners were often moved to tears by the beauty, originality, and high emotion of his playing, as well as its indefinable "magical quality";[1] the idea of hearing Beethoven play remains a tantalizing fantasy of music lovers to this day. He was not, however, a flawless technician, from most accounts; others played more smoothly, and with greater polish. And of course, his playing probably deteriorated, as did the maintenance of his pianos,[2] once deafness began to envelop him.

In Beethoven's lifetime the piano was not the instrument we know today, but a more fragile device, still under development. Its action and sound were lighter, and its range was narrower, meaning it didn't have notes as low or as high as those of the modern piano. Sometimes, especially in the early sonatas, Beethoven composed right up to the top or bottom of the keyboard, resulting in some awkwardness that most players today adjust for by using the notes Beethoven clearly would have employed had they been available to him. Once manufacturers began to build bigger pianos, Beethoven wrote for those instruments. The "Hammerklavier" piano, for example, clearly has a larger range than that of the Op. 10 sonatas, composed twenty years earlier. In 1818 the English maker Broadwood gave Beethoven a piano which he claimed to love, though he was already quite deaf when he got it; and in 1825 he acquired another from the Viennese maker Graf with a six and one-half octave range—exactly that of a modern piano.[3] Those interested in learning more about this practical aspect of Beethoven's creativity would do well to read "The Limits of Beethoven's Keyboard" in Charles Rosen's study *Beethoven's Piano Sonatas: A Short Companion*.[4]

Music critics have carved Beethoven's oeuvre into three periods, referred to as early, lasting until about 1800; middle, which in terms of the works for piano lasts until about 1816; and late, which includes everything from then up to his death in 1827. The classification of Beethoven's music into these three broad eras works well, with perhaps one exception.

Joyful energy and frank expression characterize the early works of the young master, which, while undoubtedly influenced by his predecessors—chiefly Haydn and Mozart, but a host of others, too—still show Beethoven's forcefulness and desire to stretch and alter the musical forms he inherited. There is nothing immature or unsatisfying about the early works, which for the purpose of our survey covers the sonatas from Op. 2, published in 1796, through Op. 28, of 1801, as well as the First and Second Piano Concertos. The ambitious novice listener may well be startled by how rich these fifteen early sonatas are. Other well-known works from Beethoven's first period include the Trios for Piano, Violin, and Cello Op. 1; the Sonatas for Violin and Piano Opp. 12, 23, and 24; the six String Quartets Op. 18; and the First and Second Symphonies.

Beethoven intensified the expression of struggle already present in his music while continuing to strain against the limits of form, expanding nearly every musical structure he touched. Though deafness now encroached, Beethoven's personal problems seem to have had remarkably little effect on his creative life: he simply willed the change in his style. Characteristic of his music from this middle period are a significant expansion in the dimensions of the pieces, an intensification of rhythmic energy, and, crucially, a sense of epic conflict set forth at the very beginning of a work, settled decisively and emphatically at its end. That outcome is often triumphant, as in the famous Symphony No. 5; or it may be tragic, as in the "Appassionata" Sonata. Beethoven composed much of his most famous music in his middle period, including the Third through Seventh Symphonies; his only opera, *Fidelio*; and much chamber music, including the String Quartets Opp. 59 and 74, and several of the sonatas for violin and piano. The solo piano music of the middle period includes the nine sonatas from Op. 30 through Op. 81a (excluding the two little sonatas of Op. 49, which were written earlier), all of the important sets of variations for piano except for the *Diabelli*, and the Bagatelles Op. 33. The Third, Fourth, and Fifth Piano Concertos all belong to this most famous and popular phase of the composer's career.

But Beethoven didn't work entirely for the convenience of musicologists and historians. From roughly 1812 to 1818 he endured a period of relatively low productivity, composing only a few notable works that fit comfortably into neither the middle nor the late periods. These include the final sonata for violin and piano, Op. 96, which, although dating from 1812, has a whiff of late-period ecstasy; the sublime song cycle *An die ferne Geliebte*, Op. 98, of 1816; and the pair of difficult-to-grasp Sonatas for Cello and Piano Op. 102, of 1814. Nor does the brilliant neoclassical Symphony No. 8, Op. 93, of 1812 fit the middle-period mold. Two important piano sonatas belong to this intermediate period: Op. 90, with its strange, terse opening movement, and Op. 101, perhaps the hardest of the whole series to get to know and one of the most challenging to play as well. Wildly various in style, the works of this phase do not take well to broad categorization, except perhaps that one may discern in them a greater concentration, and in some, at least, a departure from the gigantism of the middle period.

Beethoven ended his dry spell—and did writers about music a favor—with a bang, completing the titanic "Hammerklavier" Sonata, Op. 106, in 1818, and opening what his followers would view as his late period. We will look at this mighty and terrifying work in chapter 9. It represents a violent breakthrough to a new style: the triumphalism of the middle period has yielded to a more ambivalent posture in which the composer has learned to embrace his suffering and to yield creatively to it. The music of this period, all composed when he was completely deaf, is infinitely complex, profound, sometimes even mellow—and various in size and scope. Beethoven is abrupt, rapturous, and as harmonically rich as ever, but more reliant on counterpoint and variation form. Struggle continues, as for example in Op. 106 or the first movement of Op. 111, but any "victory" you may hear at the end of a late-period work will bear little resemblance to that in a predecessor of fifteen or twenty years earlier.

The works for piano are few but choice: the "Hammerklavier," followed by the grand final trilogy of sonatas, Opp. 109, 110, and 111; the Bagatelles Opp. 119 and 126, abrupt and deep; and the *Diabelli Variations*, Op. 120. The composer's attention was also focused on the largest works he ever wrote, the Symphony No. 9 and the *Missa Solemnis*, a vast, thorny setting of the Catholic mass. The scale of many—though not all—of these works is huge. The crowning jewels of Beethoven's work are the five string quartets he completed in the years before his death, in order of composition: E-flat Major, Op. 127; A Minor, Op. 132; B-flat Major, Op. 130; the Grosse Fuge, or Great Fugue, Op. 133 (a colossal finale intended for Op. 130 that was later recast as a separate work); C-sharp Minor, Op. 131; and F Major, Op. 135. All are stupendous, but the C-sharp Minor Quartet is like nothing else in this world, a lyrical, seven-movement outpouring of Beethoven's

mature tragic vision. And in the F Major Quartet, he moves on, miracu-
lously, with a wonderful work in a comic vein—rather like what Verdi
would later do, wrapping up his career as an operatic composer with
Otello, then the comedy *Falstaff*.

A Few Matters of Form

Beethoven has a well-deserved reputation as a master of form. From the
earliest works examined in this survey he displays a command of structure that allows him to shape them toward his own expressive ends,
rather than to follow rules for their own sake. As he grew artistically,
his formal skills grew commensurately, a key element of his mastery.
Beethoven subjected even his wildest ideas, like those of the Bagatelle,
Op. 33 No. 7 (track 3 on the CD accompanying this book), or the first
movement of the "Waldstein" Sonata (CD Track 4) to rigorous musical
structures; the tension between the composer's potent material and his
stern adherence to form is a key source of Beethoven's power. This book
emphasizes Beethoven's formal procedures because they provide such
clear road maps to the music. Therefore, since the names of Beethoven's
forms necessarily come up again and again, a few words to define and
describe them are in order.

Within the varied group that the sonatas make up, **sonata form**
is dominant. But it's important to understand that this is an abstract
term. It describes a structure that Beethoven used in other instrumental works, including all his works for chamber ensembles, concertos,
and the symphonies, not just for sonatas. The structure, as Beethoven
inherited it from Haydn, Mozart, and others, has three parts: first
comes the **exposition**, in which the themes or thematic groups are
set forth. In general, these themes present contrasting characters, with
the opening one usually being strong or "masculine" and the second
lyrical or "feminine." (But not necessarily: thematic characters are
readily and often reversed.) The exposition is then typically repeated.
It's followed by the **development** section (sometimes known as the
"working-out"), in which the themes are picked apart, placed into conflict, recombined, and put through some changes of key. Then follows

the **recapitulation**, in which the opening material is restated, usually in expanded form, occasionally compressed, but almost never literally; the wanderings of the development reveal the material in a new light. There's also often a closing section called a **coda** (from the Latin *cauda*, "tail") of varying length. Beethoven's tendency to emphasize the endings of his movements grew more pronounced over the course of his career, and his codas grew longer and took on more importance and expressive weight.

Sonata form is a term Beethoven himself didn't use, and the outline above gives only the most basic sense of how it functions. Haydn typically used short themes, then bent and fractured them, misleading the listener's ear rhythmically or harmonically—or both—from the expected trajectories; Mozart wove longer themes into a kind of lyric drama. Beethoven borrowed both approaches from his predecessors, but also changed the nature of the form in his own manner, often deploying short, pithy, nonmelodic themes known as **mottoes** into more violent conflict. Again, these are generalizations: all three masters were ambitious and easily bored, and they welcomed the challenge of altering and expanding the forms in which they worked.

Like Haydn and Mozart, Beethoven never used sonata form the same way twice, expanding and subtilizing it as he worked. It's crucial to understand two things about this form. The first is its nature as an arena for a musical discussion, for dialectic, and occasionally for battle. The second is that sonata-form movements are found at the opening of a multimovement instrumental work, and, as with the first acts of stage dramas, the tensions they generate must then be resolved by the remaining sections.

Beethoven often used **ABA** or **tripartite form** for his slow movements. It is a three-part (hence tripartite) form in which the two outer sections set a generously proportioned melody that's operatic, hymnlike, or songlike in nature with a contrasting middle section. "ABA" is merely shorthand describing the structure, with A representing the outer sections and B the middle. The form itself is presumably a descendant or offshoot of the *da capo* arias of the baroque era, which are built the same way. Beethoven might make the middle contrast far more dramatically with the opening material than baroque composers did, and he inevitably varies the A section on its return. He also adds codas, from brief to vast.

The third movements of high classical–era instrumental works inevitably carry two of the three titles **Menuetto**, **Scherzo**, and **Trio**. "Menuetto" is of course the Italian name for the minuet, the aristocratic dance in 3/4 time. Virtually all the symphonic and chamber works by Haydn and Mozart have minuets, as do Beethoven's earliest works in sonata form. Minuets had three parts: an opening strain, a contrasting middle section, and finally a return of the opening section. In its earliest days, when played as an actual dance, the middle section was performed by three instruments and was therefore referred to as the "trio." The name stuck, though not the orchestration.

As early as 1795, with the first of his published works, the Piano Trio No. 1, Op. 1 No. 1, Beethoven had begun to employ as third movements in his instrumental works a character piece called a scherzo,[5] meaning "joke," in place of the menuetto. In the Op. 2 sonatas of the following year, No. 1 in F Minor has a menuetto, but Nos. 2 and 3 have scherzos. Although the scherzo maintained its predecessor's 3/4 time signature, Beethoven's scherzos lack the minuet's good breeding. Indeed, many are rough or even downright violent. This was an influential move, and most of the important composers after him who wrote sonatas used scherzos, which still contain a contrasting middle section called a trio. Beethoven himself didn't give up on the minuet entirely, using one as late as Op. 31 No. 3 of 1802 and as the opening movement of the eccentric and singular Op. 54, but scherzos dominate. Beethoven also switched the position of scherzo and slow movement when doing so improved the four-movement structure as a whole, as for example in the "Hammerklavier" Sonata or the Ninth Symphony.

Based, interestingly, on a verse form, the **rondo** consists of a main theme stated at the outset, alternating with nonrecurring contrasting episodes, with the main theme appearing again last. Therefore, if the main theme is A, a rondo is structured ABACA. Rondos always appear as last movements of instrumental compositions such as sonatas and symphonies. Beethoven inherited the rondo from his predecessors and developed it into a movement of great dimension and force in the sonatas, concertos, and as independent compositions. To give the rondo greater substance, he also created large-scale, complex blends of rondo and sonata form. But because the rondo typically has a playful side, Beethoven experimented with other forms, including variations, fugues, and hybrids of his own invention in its place as he placed more expressive weight on finales. Nevertheless, he employed rondo form to the very end of his career.

The self-defining title of **variations** makes a description nearly superfluous, but the variation form was so important to Beethoven that a few words seem in order. In variations, a composer takes a theme and subjects it to a series of changes that may be superficial, like decorations of the melody, or more profound, such as harmonic and contrapuntal mutations. (Counterpoint is the musical style in which individual lines have equal importance and seem to pursue each other; Bach is considered its greatest practitioner.) The theme, which invariably has a strong, memorable melodic profile, remains more or less recognizable throughout. The themes of some of Beethoven's important sets are in **binary** form, which means that they are in two parts, reaching a point of tension at the end of the first half, to which the second half then replies. Other themes are in three parts, including that of Op. 34 and the variation movement that opens the Op. 26 sonata. Beethoven's variations, like most of Mozart's, generally follow a French pattern in which the second-to-last variation is in a slow tempo and lavishly decorated, setting up for a final variation that's long, also florid, and virtuosic.[6] This also reinforces the composer's lifelong drive to add substance to his finales, and Beethoven's four important independent sets for keyboard—those discussed in chapter 12—are rear-end loaded in one way or another. There's also often a minor-key variation. Finally, over the course of the work Beethoven moves further and further from his theme, a tendency he takes to the extreme in the *Diabelli Variations*.

The **cadenza** is a showy passage, filled with fast runs and other obvious difficulties, for a solo instrument in a concerto. Usually placed right before the end of a movement, it reached its most elaborate, ritualized form in the classical era. The solo player was expected to improvise a cadenza for a minute or so on themes from the movement in a way that displayed his or her skill and taste. Of course, these varied from player to player, and great pianist-composers, including Beethoven and

Mozart, wrote and published cadenzas for their own concertos, but even today pianists often use their own. Beethoven's Piano Concerto No. 5 contains cadenzas that are written into the score and must not be substituted by others. Some of the sonatas, the C Major, Op. 2 No. 3, and the "Waldstein," for instance, feature cadenza-like passages, too.

You will see throughout this book Beethoven's works referred to by **opus**—abbreviated **Op.**—numbers. *Opus* is a Latin word that simply means "work"; its plural is abbreviated **Opp.** Like many composers, Beethoven assigned sequential opus numbers to his important works as they were published, which also make convenient handles for the individual pieces. It's standard practice in musical writing and criticism to refer to Beethoven's works by opus number; it's also easier than referring to the pieces by their full titles. You'll soon get the hang of it and see how well it works. Low numbers, from 1 through about 30, generally refer to early or early-period works. Opus numbers from 30 to about 90 are mostly for middle-period pieces, though here and after the numbers aren't an infallible guide, because some early works were published out of sequence. Opus numbers in the 90s up to 106—the "Hammerklavier" Sonata—belong to the transitional phase leading to the late period. Anything above that—the Sonatas Opp. 106, 109, 110, and 111, and the *Diabelli Variations*, Op. 120—are definitively late period.

Some Aspects of Beethoven's Life

Creative men and women fascinate us because what they produce strikes us as heroic, but it is their efforts that are prodigious, rather than their public lives. Watching even a great composer like Beethoven at work would probably grow tedious to most people before long, the artist's struggles with material and form remaining haughtily private processes on which even the best biographies can only speculate. Under the strain of work, great artists must be self-involved and rarely are conventionally "nice"; so, it appears, was Beethoven, his native awkwardness amplified by deafness.

The deafness that overtook Beethoven as he reached artistic maturity in his late twenties is inevitably the paradox that dominates the minds of his admirers when considering his life. It seems inconceivable that a deaf musician could produce work of such beauty, complexity, and depth—miraculous for us, but terrible to imagine for the man himself. Beethoven's deafness makes him the most vivid and heroic composer to us, but apart from that handicap, his life and work probably differed little from that of other composers in their outlines and essence. Since the survey format of this book allows for only a brief biographical sketch and many fine biographical studies are available,[1] what follows is an overview.

Beethoven was baptized in Bonn, in what is now Germany, on December 17, 1770, and is presumed to have been born on the day before to Johann van Beethoven and his wife, Maria Magdalena. Johann's father, whose name was originally Louis but was later Germanicized to Ludwig, was born in Mechelen, in what is now Belgium, which accounts for the Flemish tang of the "van" in the family name. This Louis/

Ludwig was a good singer and keyboard player, as was his son Johann. But neither father nor grandfather displayed talent that anticipated the magnitude of their descendant's, as in the Bach or Mozart families. Maria Magdalena was a Bonn native of deeply serious character whom the composer revered, and from whom he presumably inherited his own earnest manner.

Most of the composer's early musical training was at the hand of his father, who was evidently severe, even with a pupil of Beethoven's youth and gifts. He performed in public as early as 1778, apparently in the hope that he would be viewed as a second Mozart, the child prodigy and income machine for his own family in the 1760s. This Beethoven was not; nor was his father an astute promoter and businessman like Leopold Mozart. But like Mozart, Beethoven was in the public eye from early on. In 1780 or thereabouts he began his training with Christian Gottlob Neefe, a gifted musician who put him on to Bach's *Well-Tempered Clavier*. It was difficult music to grasp and to play, but it must have stimulated the young Beethoven's imagination enormously. Certainly his early study of Bach paid off enormously in the counterpoint-saturated works he wrote toward the end of his own career.

By 1782 Beethoven had begun composing. Some of his juvenile works included a number of the variations for piano mentioned in chapter 12, but he also composed three ambitious sonatas for the instrument, followed in 1785 by three quartets for piano and strings, much in Mozart's style, but with keyboard parts of notable difficulty, reflecting the composer's own skill as a player. Hoping to study with Mozart, Beethoven left Bonn for Vienna in early 1787, the trip subsidized by Max Franz, the elector, or ruler, of the little principality of which Bonn was the capital. Corroborated details of Beethoven's first visit to Vienna are unfortunately few. Despite the immense appeal of the idea of Mozart praising Beethoven's playing and saying the younger man would "give the world something to talk about," it's unclear whether Mozart and Beethoven actually met. Beethoven's description of Mozart's playing to his factually reliable pupil Carl Czerny as "fine but choppy, with no legato,"[2] does indicate at least that he heard Mozart play. But Beethoven would have to learn everything he was to absorb from Mozart by studying the music on his own.

What is clear is that Beethoven was recalled prematurely to Bonn by his mother's final illness; she died of tuberculosis on July 17, 1787. With his father sinking into alcoholism, the young Beethoven, known already for his moody, stubborn character, had to assume the dominant role in his family, which included two younger brothers, Johann and Carl. He also resumed his place Bonn's musical life, playing the viola in the court orchestra of the elector. Here he probably participated in performances of music at all quality levels, up to and including Haydn symphonies and Mozart operas. In 1790 he composed the elevated and ambitious *Cantata on the Death of Emperor Joseph II*—scarce in recordings but well worth hearing—and a slightly less fine cantata to celebrate the coronation of Joseph's successor, Leopold. Haydn saw and praised the score of one of these when passing through Bonn on his way to England. In 1792, on his way back, the older and younger masters met again, and it seems likely that Haydn accepted Beethoven as his pupil, signaling the end of Beethoven's time in his hometown.

In November of 1792 Beethoven left Bonn for Vienna to study with Haydn and make his own way as a composer. His friends inscribed a farewell album, in which the brilliant Count Waldstein (to whom the Op. 53 sonata is dedicated) wrote, "With unceasing diligence you will receive the spirit of Mozart [who had died in December 1791] from the hands of Haydn,"[3] predicting Beethoven's role as the next practitioner of musical art at its highest level. It didn't take long for Waldstein's prophecy to come true; by 1796 Beethoven was the acknowledged young master of Viennese musical life, with only Haydn as his senior. The traditional view that Beethoven's lessons with Haydn didn't go well owing to Beethoven's impatience now seems to lack nuance. As Barry Cooper points out in his biography,[4] Haydn helped Beethoven by lending him money and arranging for lessons with the highly esteemed contrapuntalist Johann Albrechtsberger before Haydn left for a second tour of England in early 1794. For his part, Beethoven paid for coffee and chocolate for himself and Haydn.

The years leading to and just after 1800 were productive in all ways for Beethoven, who built his reputation as a brilliant pianist and a fiery composer of genius in Vienna's lively musical scene. Performances were typically given either at public concert halls, as pioneered by Mozart, or in the private music salons of the nobility. As a great pianist, Beethoven was sought by the aristocracy, whose financial support he required but whom he resented and treated roughly—but then, he treated everyone roughly at times. The typical concerts of the time would shock a modern listener, for they consisted of movements of concertos and symphonies, which, even at their premieres, were interspersed with improvisations, or even arias from popular operas of the day. In any case, performances by Beethoven remained hot tickets until deafness ended his career as a pianist.

It used to be a commonplace of Beethoven biographies that he was the first composer to free himself from the bonds of aristocratic patronage. In fact, Mozart took the plunge before Beethoven; and our hero, although in no one's employ, was financially dependent on wealthy and aristocratic patrons. Like Mozart, he resented his position bitterly, but he was unable to hide his resentment. To a great extent, Beethoven's renowned independence was really an elaborate pretense to protect his touchy pride; thus, dedications of works to the nobility were generally rewarded with cash gifts of appreciation in return.[5] In one remarkable instance, Beethoven dedicated the great String Quartet in C-sharp Minor, Op. 131, in gratitude to Baron von Stutterheim, whose regiment the composer's nephew Karl joined in 1826, much to Beethoven's relief.

But one name—that of the Archduke Rudolph—stands out among the various barons, counts, and princesses who received dedications of important works. A member of the Austrian royal family, the son and brother of Austrian emperors, Rudolph was a very big fish as patrons went, and a composition student of Beethoven's as well. That Rudolph selected Beethoven as his teacher demonstrates the composer's preeminence in the Austrian musical universe. Among the works dedicated to Rudolph are (unsurprisingly) the "Archduke" Trio, Op. 97; the Fourth and Fifth Piano Concertos; three piano sonatas, Opp. 81a (a musical testimony to Beethoven's friendship with the Archduke, covered in chapter 8), 106, and 111; and, to celebrate Rudolph's installation as archbishop of Olmütz in 1820, the *Missa Solemnis*, although Beethoven didn't complete the mass until 1822. The mild-mannered Rudolph was apparently a talented pianist and musician.[6] He was also well suited temperamentally to study with the excitable Beethoven, who seems in this one instance to have controlled his temper, probably in view of his student's rank as well as knowing how much the archduke-archbishop had done and could do on his behalf. Which, indeed, was considerable: Rudolph was one of three nobles who in 1809 endowed a fund to keep Beethoven in Vienna when Napoleon's brother offered him a job elsewhere. But genuine warmth does appear to have developed between the unlikely pair.

Beethoven published his first important works, the Piano Trios Op. 1 and the Piano Sonatas Op. 2. The composer always reserved opus numbers for the works he considered most important, though he wrote many others for quick income; as a respected composer, Beethoven was able to sell anything and everything he wrote. But the important works composed in the fertile years of his first period are many and astonishing. Beethoven strove for and achieved mastery in the instrumental genres he inherited from Haydn and Mozart, including of course the keyboard sonata and concerto, the string quartet (with the six of Op. 18, completed in 1800), and the symphony, of which the First and Second are magnificent examples of the high-classical style. No such description can be applied to the Third—the "Eroica"—of 1805, with which Beethoven shattered the boundaries of symphonic form and convention to create one of the great disruptive works in music and, indeed, in art.

In October of 1802 Beethoven wrote a document known as the Heiligenstadt Testament, named for the Viennese suburb where it was drafted. Beethoven kept the document, which he addressed to his brothers Carl and Johann (though Johann's name is curiously omitted throughout), and it was discovered among his papers after his death in 1827. Beethoven states in the letter that he had suffered from ringing and buzzing in his ears for six years, which puts its start back to 1797. Thus it appears almost certain that Beethoven had the torturous affliction known as tinnitus, of which ringing in the ears is the chief symptom. The cause of the illness is unknown, and physicians were of no help. By the spring of 1802 Beethoven's discomfort was so severe that the composer fled Vienna in a final attempt to cure the problem; six months later, no better, and having wrestled with and accepted his fate, he wrote this letter—as moving a confession as an artist has ever made.

He describes his love for humanity, and how his reticence in social situations has been misconstrued as misanthropy; he writes bitterly of the loss of his hearing, which faculty he had once had in the "highest perfection." And he dedicates himself and the rest of his life to his art.

Beethoven's creative life seems to have gone on unaffected, as though in a different sphere. Productivity remained undiminished, and a look at some of the works he composed in 1800, 1801, and 1802 as the crisis built tells a remarkable story: they include the Symphony No. 2; the six Op. 18 quartets; the Sonatas for Piano and Violin Opp. 23, 24, and 30, notable for their high energy and spirits; and the piano sonatas Opp. 22, 26, 27, 28, and 31, brilliant works that, with a couple of important exceptions, reflect little in the way of tragic emotion.

On the practical side, Beethoven dealt with his loss of hearing in various ways. Some of his pianos were built with amplification plates to magnify their sound. In 1816 the composer began to use an ear trumpet to try to capture conversations, but by 1818 his hearing had deteriorated so badly that he began to use conversation books. In these, Beethoven's friends and guests wrote questions and comments to which the composer replied verbally. Many concern mundane matters, while others offer tantalizing, one-sided discussions about musical art. Again and again, however, these methods reveal Beethoven's endless isolation. Its most terrible manifestation, well known and attested to, took place during the premiere in 1824 of the Ninth Symphony, which Beethoven nominally conducted while the orchestra secretly watched another leader. At the end of the second movement or the finale—it's unclear which—the audience broke into wild applause. Lost in his score, his back to the crowd, Beethoven had to be turned by one of the singers to face the cheering.

Deafness was far from Beethoven's only health problem, though it was of course the most crippling. He was prone to digestive and abdominal ailments, as well, and seems to have died of liver disease, intestinal disease—possibly colitis—and kidney failure at a relatively young fifty-six, old though he looked. He suffered from a variety of illnesses for the last ten years of his life, yet worked on, composing some of his greatest music in the wake of his physical suffering. The A-flat Major Sonata, Op. 110, of 1821 (which we will look at in chapter 10), composed after bouts with rheumatism and jaundice, is a work of profound beauty and a sense of ever-rising strength. The most notable example of his direct musical response to recuperation, from an even more serious illness suffered in 1825, is the sublime slow movement of the A Minor String Quartet, Op. 132, which he subtitled "Holy Song of Thanksgiving to the Deity by a Convalescent, in the Lydian Mode."

Beethoven's mental health raises other questions. His temperament was difficult even when he was young, well, and able to hear; deafness only exacerbated his natural touchiness, moodiness, and suspiciousness. Deafness also threw his eccentricity into high relief, making it easy for the vulgar to call him crazy. That Beethoven's music was the most advanced of its day and consequently laden with difficulties allowed some musicians, including fine ones such as the composer Carl Maria von Weber, to question his sanity, too;[7] but it seems to have been widely accepted in the musical community that Beethoven was a pioneer, "composing for the future." And in spite of his often troublesome personality, Beethoven had close friendships to the end, with some who knew him well speaking of his high-mindedness, even, remarkably, calling him a greater man than artist.[8] Even deaf, Beethoven had charisma and what seems to have been a genuine sweetness, always tempered by bluntness, that held the loyalty of a small inner circle.

Certainly nothing underscores Beethoven's personal awkwardness with greater clarity than his painfully clumsy attempts to dominate the lives of his family. As the oldest of three surviving siblings, he felt free to dictate to his two brothers in all matters, imposing his own genuinely high morals on two average men who chafed under the burden. Carl's marriage to Johanna Reiss in 1806 against Beethoven's wishes, and the composer's litigation to deprive Johanna of her maternal rights after Carl's death in 1815, are covered in detail in other biographical studies, but the story shows the composer at his most aggressive—although, ironically, his harsh assessment of Johanna's character was on target. Later, Beethoven's suffocating love for his nephew Karl drove the poor, ordinary youth straight back to his mother and finally, in 1826, to attempt suicide. All these events display the composer's lack of emotional moderation, and all may have taken a toll on his physical well-being.

Beethoven had an active, if apparently chaste, love life that has been the subject of endless study and speculation. He loved women, and some were inevitably attracted to him, but he never married and was not a seducer, which his personal morality forbade.[9] He fell in love many times: one of his early loves was one Magdalena Willman, also from Bonn, to whom he proposed in 1795, presumably in Vienna, but who turned him down "because he was so ugly and half crazy."[10] Many of his loves were aristocrats, just above his station, to whom he taught piano, or married women. A number of commentators have suggested that the composer was attracted to women who weren't available to him for one reason or another, because he knew that solitude was essential to the fulfillment of his art. It makes sense that he never married because he was too busy to share his life with someone else, but he suffered terribly from loneliness as a result.

In 1812 Beethoven wrote a passionate letter to a woman addressed only as "Immortal Beloved," which was found, unsent like the Heiligenstadt Testament, among his papers after his death. This letter has by itself spawned a whole industry, including books and a film or two, to identify the woman to whom it was addressed, but the best recent scholarship suggests—there is no absolute certainty—that she was Antonie Brentano. This Vienna native returned to her hometown with her husband from Frankfurt between 1809 and 1812, when she and Beethoven would have come to know one another. Brentano is, indeed, one of those who wrote warmly of Beethoven the man. But Beethoven had to renounce her, and the idea of conjugal love. This seems to have been his last serious love, and its end coincides with the start of the six-year drop-off in his output, from 1812 to 1817.

Beethoven did not stop composing during this period; indeed, he wrote many wonderful works over these years, but there are fewer, and they are generally smaller in scale than those either of the immensely fertile period before or the one that would follow starting in 1817. One project he undertook was the revision in 1814 of his opera *Fidelio* into its final form, no small task. And many of the works of the period, while stylistically various—the Piano Sonatas Opp. 90 and 101; the Sonatas for Cello and Piano Op. 102; the Tenth (and last) Sonata for Piano and Violin, Op. 96; and the song cycle *An die ferne Geliebte*, Op. 98—

are hardly insignificant. It is, of course, impossible to know why the master's creative engine downshifted for six years. It would be easy to blame the illness and death of his brother Carl and his subsequent legal battle with Johanna for custody of their son Karl, but Beethoven had always been able to deal with all kinds of personal business while composing without his productivity suffering in the least. And he continued to deal with the same difficult matters once the tide of inspiration rose again in 1817 with the "Hammerklavier" Sonata, Op. 106, ending the apparent creative drought.

Over the years, Beethoven had developed methods of stimulating his imagination by improvising at the keyboard and, in later years, keeping sketchbooks at hand at all times, even by his bedside, so that he could jot down ideas as they came or work more extensively on material as he took his daily walks. Tales of his humming and howling as he worked through an idea are common in his biographies. And once a work was in process, everything else took second place. Students waited or were dismissed without their lessons and meals were skipped until Beethoven was satisfied that the process had run its course.[11] A young friend's recollection is deeply revealing:

> He was once expected for dinner with us, and it was getting close to two, our dinner-time. My parents feared, with good reason, that he might have got deep into composing and forgotten all about the time, and sent me over to fetch him. I found him at his desk, facing the open door to the piano room, writing one of the last (Galitzin) quartets. He looked up and told me to wait a bit, until he had put his idea down on paper. I was quiet for a while and then went over to the Graf piano (with the added amplifying apparatus), which was nearest, and began to strum lightly on the keys, not being convinced that Beethoven was deaf to musical tones.... He heard nothing, and kept on writing, unconcerned, until finally he was finished and came out with me.[12]

While demonstrating the depth of Beethoven's deafness in his last years, Gerhard von Breuning's story shows a methodical artist at work—more disciplined athlete than wild-eyed visionary, even while composing visionary music. Certainly Beethoven suffered in the act of creation, but it also brought him immense pleasure and a profound joy.

The First, Second, and Third Concertos
Under Mozart's Influence

Beethoven's five concertos for piano and orchestra stand among his most important large-scale compositions and have always been enormously popular. Beethoven composed the first three as vehicles for his own performances, but he seems not to have played No. 3 more than once or twice. He played the Concerto No. 4 once or possibly twice, in 1807 and 1808, and never played the popular No. 5 of 1809 because of the deterioration of his hearing. This work is Beethoven's last in the concerto form, his loss of interest apparently coinciding with the end of his own career as a performer.[1]

The concerto of the classical era is a large-scale work, usually in three movements, in which a soloist (most commonly a pianist or violinist) plays with an orchestra. Virtuoso displays are typically part of the soloist's role; the concerto is a kind of mini-opera where the solo instrument acts in place of the human voice, "singing" eloquently, passionately, and wittily against the orchestra, which, representing the outside world, would dominate the individual, as symbolized by the soloist. This definition is a fairly crude simplification: there are many moments in all concertos when solo and orchestra play in pleasing and complex dialogue. But at its heart, the popular concerto of the classical and romantic eras is an artfully managed musical conflict between the individual and the crowd.

The instrumental concerto itself is an Italian invention, brought to an early peak by Arcangelo Corelli in his works for violin accompanied by a small string orchestra, and by Vivaldi in works for an astonishingly wide range of solo instruments and strings. (A steady back-and-forth interplay between the solo instrument and small orchestra is a charac-

teristic of baroque concertos.) The energetic concerto style fascinated
Bach, who transcribed a number of Vivaldi's concertos and wrote the
Italian Concerto, a glittering take-off, for solo harpsichord. The history
of the keyboard concerto as a form does not predate Beethoven's era
by much: J. S. Bach's Brandenburg Concerto No. 5 of 1721, for harpsichord, flute, and violin with string orchestra, is credited as being the
first concerto for keyboard and orchestra, and Bach also wrote other
well-known keyboard concertos. Haydn wrote several, but only one,
in D major, has achieved even modest popularity. The field is justifi-
ably dominated by Mozart, whose genius for musical drama was singu-
larly suited to the drama implicit in the concerto form, bringing that
potential to the highest imaginative plane. Of Mozart's twenty-seven
keyboard concertos, at least thirteen are masterpieces, each speaking
in its own voice, with some of the last eight—No. 24 in C Minor, K.
491, No. 25 in C Major, K. 503, and No. 27 in B-flat Major, K. 595, to
list three leading candidates—standing close to the pinnacle of instrumental music of the classical era.

Mozart's influence, particularly in the first three of Beethoven's
concertos, is profound and unmistakable. Beethoven would have made
it his business to know as many of Mozart's concertos as he could hear
or read in score, if one was available—it wasn't always. Carl Czerny,
Beethoven's pupil and friend, played Mozart's K. 503 at his audition to
study with Beethoven, who sat down next to him and joined in, so he
clearly knew that concerto by heart.[2] Mozart's piano concertos blend
lyricism, drama, and wit in fleet patterns that Beethoven surely admired
but never quite achieved for himself, his concertos having thicker and
more aggressive piano writing and growing progressively larger in scale.
The early, clearly Mozartean Concerto No. 2 is a second-tier work that's
still fun to hear, and Beethoven's essays in the form seem to grow more
convincing as the composer sheds some of Mozart's influence and writes
more fully in his own monumental style, as he does in the Fourth and
Fifth Concertos.

The classical-era piano concerto that Beethoven inherited from
Mozart consists of a large opening movement in a variant of sonata
form modified to accommodate the dual presentation of thematic material by the orchestra and the solo instrument. The second movements

are slow and songful; Mozart generally favored Italianate, arialike themes. Beethoven wrote two in this style, for the First and Second Concertos, while those of the Third and Fifth are more hymnlike. The famous slow movement of the Fourth Concerto is a singular, astonishing construction of Beethoven's own. And all five concertos end, as do most of Mozart's, with Rondo movements; Beethoven's rondos grow progressively larger in scale, and that of the Fifth is immense. Thematic development occurs not only in the usual ways, but also, crucially, in how the musical material is distributed and redistributed between the solo instrument and the orchestra.

Many of Mozart's mature piano concertos open with themes based on marches, some of which, including the one that opens the famous Concerto No. 21 in C Major, K. 467, are grand. Others, however, including those that open the great pair of No. 17 in G Major, K. 453, and No. 18 in B-flat Major, K. 456, are more playful; Mozart was a great composer of marches. The ubiquity of the march seems to reflect the constant presence of the military on parade in late eighteenth-century Europe. In Beethoven's time, the Napoleonic wars were turning the military into a darker, more destructive presence,[3] as reflected in the terse, marchlike theme that opens the Concerto No. 3 in C Minor. But the opening march of Beethoven's Concerto No. 1 in C Major, Op. 15, is surely Mozartean in inspiration, with a bit more weight, typical of Beethoven's own style. Composed in 1795, Op. 15 was published before the older B-flat Major Concerto, which came out in 1801 as Op. 19.

Beethoven's concerto begins with its march theme stated, as Mozart's usually were, quietly in the strings, the low volume adding excitement and preparing the way for a louder incarnation, which follows immediately, punctuated and backed by winds. The second theme, a lyrical melody in wandering eighth notes, enters softly. The first theme returns, and the final thematic element, a fanfare for the brass and winds with a wiggling tail, rounds out the orchestral presentation. Beethoven makes much use of this humorous wiggling figure over the course of the movement. The piano enters with a new and genial theme of its own, to which the orchestra responds with fragments of the main march idea that are then embroidered by the piano. The winds chatter as the piano moves to a minor key, and finally the second theme comes in, which the piano plays in an extended version. The fanfare appears, with the piano taking the wiggling tail as a cue for an extended running passage. This leads to a memorable sequence in which the right hand plays chunky chords over rushing triplets in the left. When it soon recurs with the material reversed, it introduces a grand and loud restatement of the march by the orchestra, beginning a development-like passage in which Beethoven picks the themes apart and moves them into a few different keys (chiefly E-flat major) in a long, quiet dialogue between piano and orchestra. This ends on a series of thoughtful, even dreamy falling chords accompanied by the horns as a huge falling scale for the keyboard marks the opening of the recapitulation.

The theme is thundered out, and a discussion of the basic material, shared now between piano and orchestra, leads to that convention of the concerto that became a cliché: the cadenza. Growing out of the mania of the classical age for improvisation to let soloist weave the movement's motivic material into a long, showy passage, it begins on a huge, expectant dominant chord and leads to a final, forceful statement of the march theme.

The second movement is a very slow Largo ("broad") movement in a somewhat lopsided sonata form based on an arialike theme stated at the outset by the piano, accompanied by soft strings. The second part of the first thematic group is a rather self-consciously "sublime" reply for the orchestra over a walking bass line, followed by a lovely postlude, sung by a pair of clarinets that is perhaps Beethoven's happiest inspiration here. He seems to be following the Mozartean example of placing the liquid tone of this then-new woodwind in the orchestral forefront, as Mozart did in two of his greatest concertos, No. 22 in E-flat Major, K. 482, and No. 23 in A Major, K. 488. The clarinet's ability to sing long melodies effortlessly works well in this lyrical slow movement, where the instrument acts as a frequent companion to the solo piano. The second theme, based on a sighing idea, is far shorter and seems sketchier than the long opening sequence; moreover, Beethoven uses only the far more luxuriant first thematic group in the very short development. The piano works delicate embroidery and the orchestra remains very quiet, as it does when the rapt restatement of the opening recurs. An expanded section over a triplet accompaniment, to quiet pizzicato (plucked) strings is a nice touch, as is the piano's trill-laden accompaniment to the clarinet postlude. Then, in a long, lingering fare-well, Beethoven adds a coda of enormous proportions. A rising scale in thirds in the right hand anticipates Chopin's sound, and the long duet for piano and clarinet just before the closing bars seems to foreshadow Beethoven's more sophisticated and striking instrumental pairings in the Concerto No. 5.

The differences in the musical personalities of Beethoven and his model Mozart are evident in the superb Rondo that concludes Beethoven's Piano Concerto No. 1, perhaps the most successful por-tion of the composition. The concluding Rondo of a Mozart concerto typically opens with a weightless, lyrical theme, often in dance rhythm, presented by solo piano; it gives way to an ethereal blend of ideal-ized chorography, humor, and shadows that hint at deeper emotions beneath the surface sheen. Beethoven's Rondo for Op. 15 presents a similarity of structure, but the rougher textures and earthier mood are pure Beethoven. The opening theme, which the piano plays alone, is a gutsy theme in a strong dance rhythm, with a playful tail of squirming sixteenth notes, with which Beethoven has some fun over the course of the movement. The second part of the rondo theme is a powerful, fanfare-like theme for the horn and winds, immediately after which the piano makes an entry in more elegant spinning sixteenth notes. A third thematic feature is then introduced by the orchestra, beginning lyri-cally but ending on a more playful phrase; strongly voiced accents in the orchestral accompaniment are slightly jarring and very Beethovenian. A long, beautiful passage in which the solo piano plays with fragments of the last melody over sighing accompaniments in the winds, followed by the strings, is quietly magical. Beethoven then presents the first theme in a new rhythmic guise and to a peevish harmonic accompaniment, after which we hear it again in its original form.

The single, but highly memorable, episode follows, based on a tangy tune that may have had a "Hungarian" snap for the composer and his audience, but that sounds to modern ears very much like a samba.[4] In any case, Beethoven makes much of its jazzy swing, creating a great deal of interplay between piano and winds before working his way back to the opening thematic group. A big crescendo leads to a cadenza, then some nice shifts of harmony before a fermata (a long, deliberate pause) opens the long, splendid coda. Beethoven presents the fanfare-like theme over chuckling staccato (detached notes) strings in a delicious passage that precedes the spacious final page. Here the composer breaks the fanfare into a mock horn call for the piano, much as he would again in the Op. 81a Sonata ("Les adieux"), followed by a poetic little cadenza for the right hand. Then the oboes and horns perform a genuine wind call, and a brilliant final passage ends this satisfying and beautifully crafted Rondo movement.

As noted above, Beethoven's Piano Concerto No. 2 in B-flat Major, Op. 19, is the first he composed, but it wasn't published until 1801, after the Op. 15 concerto, when he sold it to a publisher at a reduced price. The B-flat Major Concerto, assembled from material going back to the 1780s and revised many times over the course of the 1790s, was one of the composer's showpieces for performance. It is in Beethoven's earliest, high-classical style, in which the composer, still learning his craft, was dependent on models by Haydn, Mozart, and other, now-forgotten composers whose concerti were popular at the end of the eighteenth century. As such, it's the piano concerto in which Beethoven's own distinctive musical language and style are least in evidence. The first movement in particular features rather generic-sounding thematic material, and all three movements are almost completely conventional in structure. Nevertheless, there's still much to enjoy in this lively early work.

The opening theme is a brisk gesture, a vigorous figure in a dotted (long-short) rhythm, followed by a sighing reply. A list of instrumental works from the classical era opening this way would be very long; so significant is this kind of thematic idea that it carried through Beethoven's oeuvre even to the immense and forward-looking "Hammerklavier" Sonata, Op. 106, of 1817 (covered in chapter 9), which opens with a titanic version of the same kind of theme. A stabbing phrase in the violins followed by a sharp downward pull is the next important element; then comes a more suave melody in eighth notes. An excited theme in which the violins press ahead in agitated *tremolandi* backed by the wind chords rounds off the opening thematic complex. The piano enters with a relaxed phrase that seems to comment on what went before without quoting it literally. The stabbing theme then appears, and the piano chases it, employing a combination of opening materials.

Finally, the second theme, a gracious, broader melody that combines long notes with more fluid runs, appears in the orchestra, with the piano replying at once. Now Beethoven drops the volume and modulates an extended version of the second theme unexpectedly into a cool and faraway D-flat major, an effect that looks ahead to his bolder harmonic journeys, before working back to the opening rhythm, set forth by the left hand beneath brilliant runs in the right. This rambling through remote keys is very much like a development, but that section does not actually begin until the piano repeats its thoughtful opening phrase. This section is notable for Beethoven's interesting reinterpretation of the stabbing figure into a delicate dialogue for piano and winds, then strings, as a canvas on which to carry out a shifting harmonic fabric entirely typical of these passages where thematic ideas are interchanged and transformed. Of course, the roaming leads inevitably back home to a restatement of the stiff but energetic opening idea, amplified by fuller orchestral textures and a running commentary, usually in triplets, for the piano. The recapitulation leads to a cadenza and a few concluding bars.

A serious, arialike idea opens the second movement, a good example of a classical Adagio. Note when you listen how the run on which the piano enters imitates a figure for the violins that preceded it. The second theme, more figural punctuation than a fully developed contrasting melody, enters after the piano's long initial statement. Some twisting figures in the lower strings mimic the long runs for the violins and piano that came before and also add fullness to the orchestral texture. The most remarkable passage comes at the heart of the movement, where winds chant the opening theme ecstatically above pizzicato strings, to which the piano adds a billowing accompaniment in rapid, broken figuration. Beethoven deploys a similar concept more elaborately in the second movement of the next concerto, in C minor. When reiterating the opening ideas, Beethoven extends the phrases luxuriously, adding enriched virtuosic figuration including trills and a recitative-like passage for the piano marked *con gran espressione*, as though unwilling to end the movement. The piano is silent as the orchestra, led by the winds, solemnly sings the opening theme to conclude this lovely and well-made lyrical essay.

The strong profiles of the three main themes of the rondo that concludes the concerto (CD Track 1) make it the most memorable movement of the whole piece. Beethoven also employs the various aspects of the flexible 6/8 time signature to vary the material and give it a delicacy reminiscent of Mozart's concerto finales. The movement opens with the main theme stated by the solo piano. Energetic and cheerful, the lilting tune imprints easily on the mind. The second of the rondo's chief themes enters at 0:26, a falling figure in a slower rhythm, to which the piano responds playfully. A long series of scales over excited murmuring in the strings (0:47) leads to the final element in the rondo themes, another springy and memorable melody stated by the solo piano at 0:55. From 1:05 to 1:32, piano and orchestra trade ideas, with the winds chortling in the background. At 1:40 the scales return but seem to hesitate, as though looking for direction. But the harmonic journey resumes as the opening theme is restated at 1:51.

The single episode, based on a bounding figure in the complementary key of G minor, begins at 2:25, with an interesting syncopated descent of the theme at 2:42, followed by leaping thirds (2:55). Again, Beethoven treats this second theme as though it has lost its way before reprising the rondo theme at 3:18. At 3:58 the piano plays a swift, enchanting version of the lilting theme, which now comes back in a new guise, mixed with fleeting scales and interspersed with interjections from the orchestra (4:13–4:36). The scales resume, again as though having lost direction (5:20), when Beethoven moves abruptly but quietly into the remote key of G major, of which note the magical effect. He maneuvers deftly back to B-flat major, however, for the fourth and final statement of the rondo theme (5:13). That leads immediately into the coda at 5:22. Listen for the difficult-to-execute descending thirds at 5:28 and for the equally difficult double trill in the right hand at 5:57, leading to the soloist's gentle final notes, picked up by the orchestra at 6:16, and the closing cadences.

Serious and exciting, the Piano Concerto No. 3 in C Minor, Op. 37, is a popular repertory staple. It's a strong middle-period work, distinctive for its scale and force as well as for its place in the circle of works in Beethoven's signature key. Interestingly, the precise date of its composition is uncertain; recent research places its composition to 1802 and early 1803, although the composer had sketched ideas for the work for years before.[5] He performed it for the first time on April 5, 1803, at a long concert of his own works that also included the First and Second Symphonies and the oratorio *Christus am Ölberge* (Christ on the Mount of Olives). The dramatic affect of the Third Concerto marks a complete departure from the cheerful high classicism of its two predecessors. Gloomy concertos in minor keys were rare at the time,[6] with only Mozart's two majestic forays (D Minor, K. 466, and C Minor, K. 491) as likely models for Beethoven. Certainly Mozart's great concerto in C minor seems to cast a shadow over Beethoven's Op. 37, especially in the first movement, where the opening themes are markedly similar; and the rondo that concludes Mozart's D Minor Concerto might well have influenced Beethoven when composing the finale to the present work.

The similarity in the opening ideas of Mozart's and Beethoven's C Minor Concertos will be clear if you listen in succession to the opening minute or so both. Both begin with a C minor chord broken into its three rising notes, C, E-flat, and G, played in the identical rhythm, and the next note, a G, is the same, too. But Mozart's time signature is 3/4, while Beethoven's is a marchlike 4/4. Mozart's theme arches off gracefully into a long twelve-bar phrase, while Beethoven's ends tensely in four bars, in a snapping rhythm reminiscent of two drumbeats (short-long, short-long), which idea dominates the movement. Both concertos also feature drums and trumpets in their scoring.

The winds reply to the opening motive with an echo that brackets rather than extends the phrase, and the full orchestra makes a somber reply with a falling thematic element. Additional phrases, separated by pauses, pass like characters in a drama, but all are serious, even grim, until a melting but dignified tune in E-flat major, led by the clarinets, appears about one and a half minutes in. But the consolation provided by this stately theme is short-lived, and Beethoven pulls back to the minor key and dramatic, conflict-driven thematic elements. The piano enters on fierce runs that sweep up the keyboard, then states the opening theme aggressively. What follows is a development, led by the piano, with orchestral commentary as the horns, then the clarinets and bassoons, then the strings take up the drumbeat rhythm in a powerful and effective redistribution. A stabbing element from the opening group is then heard, intensifying the sense of tragedy and conflict. The winds moan as the piano decorates thematic fragments over a quiet but steady pulse in the strings, and the short-long drum motto echoes again and again across the orchestral background, finally taken up by the timpani. Broken chords for the piano over moaning winds and the drum rhythm in the strings follow as the composer makes his way back to a loud and ferocious restatement of the opening theme for the full orchestra.

The recapitulation is notable for some interesting sonic interplay as the solo piano plays broken octaves in a high register against the piping of the flutes and oboes. The syncopated passage that leads to the cadenza has a terrible intensity, and the orchestra's quiet pick-up, with the drumbeat figure, at the cadenza's end is striking and effective for its contrast with the loud passage that came before. The cadenza generally performed, by the way, is Beethoven's own, and quite grand. The piano picks up the short-long drumbeat figure and extends it into an impassioned five-note phrase. Heavy repeated notes bang the movement shut.

In Arthur Rubinstein's 1944 live recording of the C Minor Piano Concerto with the NBC Symphony under Toscanini, the pianist strikes the opening chord of the second movement almost as soon as the sound of the final notes of the first movement have died away, with only the briefest pause. This is crucial because it highlights the contrast in between the dark C minor tonality of the opening movement and the cool, ethereal E major of the following Largo. The two keys are almost as far apart in the structure of keys (the circle of fifths) as possible, and E major is anything but typical for a movement in a big, high-classical instrumental work in C minor. Beethoven wrote the slow movement of the Sonata No. 2 in C Major, Op. 2 No. 3, in E major (see pp. 50–52), which was daring enough; but the contrast with C minor in the concerto is even more radical. Beethoven liked to experiment with remote and even conflicting key relationships; that's part of why his music sounds modern today, and why it must have seemed advanced and even mad to his contemporaries.

And the Largo is a remarkable creation for many other reasons, too. Its very slow tempo stands in contrast with the quick speeds of the outer movements that flank it, and its meditative, ecstatic character stands utterly apart from the violence and vigor of those opening and closing movements. The piano writing is florid and intensely ornamental, while that of the outer movements is more direct and with great forward impetus. The Largo also contains a passage in which Beethoven melds piano and orchestra into an astonishing harplike sonority. The movement opens with the piano stating the hymnlike theme, some chords of which are broken into harplike arpeggios. The final section of the long melody is a more agitated figure of falling triplets over a *tremolando*, or trembling figure, in the left hand. The orchestra responds with a heart-easing reply. Note that Beethoven mutes the strings, in another tonal contrast with their bright sound in the first and last movements. The piano plays a long, elaborate passage in rapid thirds to conclude the thematic group.

The strings play an expressive phrase in a halting, syncopated rhythm to commence the great central section of the movement. Here, the piano embarks on long, murmuring arpeggios, *tremolandi*, and runs, all take-offs on the sound of the harp, while the winds sound sweet melodic fragments in dialogue; the strings hold the beat in stately pizzicati that also evoke the harp. Indistinct yet strangely eloquent, this marvelous passage paradoxically forms the ecstatic heart of a conflict-laden concerto. The movement's main theme comes back, even more elaborately decorated, as the piano adds a constant flow of commentary in the form of high-strung runs, trills, and other embroidery to the melody, now carried by the orchestra. A short but exquisite cadenza for the right hand leads to a final iteration of a fragment of the hymn-like tune, and the final E major chord, played loud, surely expresses exaltation.

The action-packed rondo opens with a memorable, driving C minor theme in a more upbeat tone that's completely different from that of the fierce opening movement. Beethoven builds in a thoughtful ritardando—a deliberate slowdown—followed by a brief cadenza at three of its four appearances over the course of the movement. One thematic element that recalls the posture of the first movement is a vehement, three-note march figure for trumpets, drums, and winds, to which the piano always replies with rising triplets, but this brief gesture lacks the intensity of the first movement's material, and therefore seems more a witty piece of affect the musical puzzle that is the rondo. The single episode, in A-flat major, is a lyrical interlude, recognizable by its presentation by the clarinets. This perhaps also recalls the first movement, where the composer used same instrument to introduce its more songful, contrasting theme. But again, the mood of this rondo seems relatively playful.

As noted, concertos in minor keys were a rarity in the classical era, with only ambitious composers like Mozart and Beethoven trying their hands at the task. In his two minor-key piano concertos, Mozart takes widely different approaches to the problem of how to end a dramatic concerto, defined by its "dark" tonality. The K. 466 concerto has a powerful D minor rondo to which the composer appends a coda in D major that sounds like an opera's cheerful closing ensemble. He pursues an altogether tougher course in the C minor concerto (K. 491), replacing the normal rondo with a sublime theme and variations that ends the work in C minor in an unambiguously tragic mode that is exceptional, and perhaps singular, for its day. Beethoven knew the D minor work, for he composed a cadenza for its first movement that virtually all performers still use. And it seems certain that he knew K. 491. In the Third Piano Concerto Beethoven adheres perhaps a bit more closely to the K. 466 model, moving to C major for the long coda (which begins with the movement's third cadenza), keeping the rondo theme as the main idea for the passage, speeding up the tempo, changing the time signature to a bouncy 6/8, and racing, almost breathlessly, to a glittering ending.

The Fourth and
Fifth Concertos

With the Fourth and Fifth Concertos, Beethoven finds his own voice. The Mozartean influences that seem so distinct in the first three works in this form are no longer particularly evident in these two majestic creations. The Fourth is one of the most original of all the master's compositions in form and expressive content, and the Fifth is an expansive work in the grand style that can't be mistaken for the work of any other composer. These two masterpieces have achieved immense and apparently imperishable popularity. Beethoven dedicated both concertos to his most important patron, the Archduke Rudolph. Probably completed in 1806, the Fourth Concerto was apparently the last of the concertos Beethoven himself played in public, on December 22, 1808, at another of those mammoth musical events that were the norm in those days. Beethoven may also have played it in March 1807 at a musicale in the home of his patron, Prince Lobkowitz.[1] The Fifth was completed in 1809 and published in 1811.

What makes the Concerto No. 4 so unusual from an analytical point of view are its divergences from conventional concerto structure, including a statement of the primary theme by the solo piano at the start of the work; a second movement that is formally *sui generis*, without precedent or heir; and some significant alterations to the rondo form in the final movement. Emotionally, the Fourth Concerto beguiles with its personal, lyrical, and poetic character, for which it stands alone among the master's works. Perhaps Beethoven's most important and experimental piece in this genre, the composer endowed the Fourth with an inwardness atypical of the concerto and a mellowness that anticipates

his late-period style, while creating for the Fourth a singular and magical sound world all its own.

The work opens unusually, as noted above, with a statement of the
main theme of the first movement by the piano. This ruminative idea,
in rich, repeated chords with a brief, rising run toward its end, ends
on a questioning phrase. The opening would seem to have little in
common with the other important piano concerto—Mozart's No. 9,
K. 271—where the piano replies immediately to the orchestra's bold
opening phrase. The character of Mozart's theme and the piano's frisky
response do not anticipate Beethoven's ineffably solemn utterance; so
although Beethoven's concept is not without Mozartean precedent, the
similarity is only of the most general sort. The orchestral reply, assigned
by Beethoven to the strings playing very softly, is a slightly extended
version of the opening idea, but in the faraway key of B major, adding
mystery to an already startling opening sequence; it's also an example
of Beethoven's interest in the nontraditional harmonic interval of the
third. But rapid travels through keys and sudden excursions to distant
tonalities, all to magical and mysterious effect, are characteristic of this
great movement. The full orchestra enters with an extended version of
the opening rhythm, nudging the harmony back through several keys to
G major. A big crescendo leads to a rather grand new idea with a sharper
rhythmic profile, which sets up another important thematic element.
Now, Beethoven lowers the volume once more—the Fourth Concerto
is a quiet work—and, over throbbing triplets for the violins, introduces
a hushed tune with a choreographic feel in the winds, underpinned by
an echoing line in the cellos and double basses playing pizzicato. This
sequence ends on a mighty upward-reaching melodic phrase that plays
an important role over the course of the movement. The opening idea
returns, in a fervent but never violent utterance by the full orchestra,
as Beethoven introduces the final thematic element, a falling sequence
in fluid sixteenth notes that passes from strings to winds and back to
the lower strings again.

Finally, the piano reenters quietly, with the opening rhythm breaking out into more activity through ever-smaller notes, culminating
first in long, grand trills for both hands, then in difficult thirds for the
right. The first theme comes back in a more urgent, panting incarna-

tion in sixteenth notes and quick triplets. But suddenly a sublime new idea in a remote key (B-flat major, for those keeping track), its long, arching melody high on the keyboard and its left-hand accompaniment far below, appears pianissimo and then vanishes, like a vision. The strings introduce a rich and soothing new melodic idea that shimmers in ambiguous harmonies before the piano scampers off with its playful short-short-long rhythmic tail. The piano dominates the next long sequence, in which the mysterious second tune is the main subject of discussion, ending in an utterance by the winds of the powerful rising melodic phrase, the piano joining the ecstatic outcry with swiftly rising triplets. An immense triple trill for the piano (two for the right hand, one for the left) leads to a lyrical rendition of the last idea by the keyboard over a slowing of the tempo, and finally Beethoven returns to a new, hesitant version of the once-steady opening idea to start the development.

Here the piano moves through several keys in quick succession—at first gently, over nearly still accompaniment from the strings. But soon, in a more agitated sequence, the orchestra plays the opening motto as the piano spins a furious descant alongside, even running an earnest contrapuntal passage. But Beethoven settles this down, letting the piano decorate the main theme as it rises powerfully toward the dominant— that expectant-sounding moment paving the way for the return to the recapitulation of the opening material in the original key. This comes with a majestic falling phrase in the orchestra, led by the horns over proud string chords. The piano hammers out the main theme *fortissimo*—very loudly—in a fierce broken pattern. And suddenly, again, Beethoven drops the volume as the key shifts as before to B major and the piano decorates the main theme in gently sparkling triplets. Once again, but just this time, the sublime theme in B-flat major reappears, then vanishes amid chattering figuration and scales, and the soothing theme follows, trailed by its bouncy tail. Beethoven now summons all the other main ideas in a fantastical parade that includes a mighty exhalation of the powerful melodic phrase over rising triplets, then, just before the cadenza, a more lyrical rendition for the piano over a gentle string accompaniment. Beethoven's cadenza seems almost Schubertian in its blend of lyricism and rhythmic impetus. And in the long coda,

Beethoven has the soloist play sweeping scales and triplets over almost obsessive iterations of the main theme by the orchestra, at first quietly and with infinite tenderness, then more and more vigorously to the end.

Although one cannot listen to the astonishing second movement of the Fourth Concerto without feeling that Beethoven is narrating something specific—that he's telling some story in music—it's also impossible, since this is a purely instrumental work, to know what that story might be. Much thought and ink have been dedicated over the years to the "subject" of the movement (Orpheus charming the Furies in Hades is probably the leading contender), but apart from the music itself, Beethoven left no clues, so all such attempts are speculative. The movement consists of a dialogue between piano and strings; the winds are silent throughout. The strings make gruff, imperious statements in a sharp, dotted (short-long) rhythm, to which the piano responds plaintively in a smoother manner; over the course of the movement, the orchestra gradually moderates its tone, and toward the end the piano dominates the dialogue, though still with a sorrowful affect.

In addition to the sharpness of the rhythm Beethoven notates, he instructs the string players that their potent figure is to played *sempre staccato*—in detached notes throughout—and for good measure places dots over each note to emphasize the jagged effect he wants. His tempo, *andante con moto*, is moderate rather than slow. The strings play a recitative-like pattern that tends to pull downward—not exactly melodic, but certainly not plain background, either; it possesses a rough grandeur. The fierce opening statement by the strings is so emphatic that it seems to brook no opposition. The piano enters, playing a quiet, noble solo that rises and falls movingly to express a well-controlled grief. The second orchestral outburst, no less vehement than the first, rises angrily toward the end before falling again. The keyboard's articulate reply moves into major tonalities, but unlike the first exchange, the strings interrupt emphatically before the phrase has ended.

For the next few exchanges, the piano and orchestra are more intimately engaged, with the strings making little two-note interjections amid the keyboard's imploring phrases. And finally, after a long, eloquent statement from the piano that ends on a beautiful triplet cadence, the strings begin to quiet down. The pace of narrative events seems to broaden as the piano takes the lead to the movement's end, first in a long sequence that rises up, then loosens into a more flowing thematic stream, with quietly plucked strings keeping the spacious rhythm of the piano's ever-widening phrase. Suddenly the piano blazes up in three long, increasingly agitated trills on rising notes, followed by a falling figure and then a two-note figure that bounces upward. But this, too, broadens and calms into a long passage resembling a cadenza but slow and sorrow-laden, ending on three cadential chords stated in a spacious rhythm. The strings come in again, very quietly, with only the cellos and double basses playing a grumbling reminiscence of their imperious opening phrase under calm, long-held chords. The piano ends the movement on an exquisite final cadence.

The rondo, which follows without pause, is an essay in forward motion and shimmering sound. It has three unusual features. First, the strings state the main theme, rather than the piano. Secondly, the rondo is based on a single theme, with a development in place of a contrasting episode. And lastly, Beethoven brings in the trumpets and drums, which were silent in the first two movements. These of course brighten and sharpen the orchestra, which sounded with a hazy, pastel quality in the first movement and was limited to the strings only in the second. But the new brass and percussion never turn thunderous, and in the finale Beethoven keeps to the restrained palette that characterizes the concerto as a whole. Indeed, as we'll see, in many passages a single quiet cello is the piano's only companion.

The main theme itself is a shuddering idea, in a clear-cut short-short-long rhythm that rises, then falls in quick patterns, stated by the strings in an excited whisper. The piano, accompanied by that solo cello playing long-held tones below, enters with a swaggering reply in a slightly syncopated rhythm in the left hand and a wiggling sixteenth-note version in the right. The soloist plays a suave concluding phrase and then the orchestra states the main theme at full volume, the piano interjecting commentary in close exchanges. A long sequence of swift passagework for the piano acts as the bridge to a dreamy tune in a languid rhythm, accompanied by a single, quiet cello far below. Set high on the keyboard, its pace differs radically from that of the rushing rondo theme; the effect is similar to that of the sublime melody of the first movement, seeming to take us far away for a moment, although the D major tonality of this tune is more closely related to the home key of G major. Soon the winds add a mellow note to the orchestral accompaniment, and before long the nervous energy of the main theme has stolen back in and, following a cadenza, resumed command of the proceedings.

The piano dominates the second iteration of the rondo theme with furious passagework as the winds scamper around; Beethoven brings back the blessed dreamy tune, first in its original shape and then, in a complete change of pace, in a profound but joyful contrapuntal guise for the orchestra. Soon, in an exquisite inspiration, the violas and solo cello play a tranquil, rhythmically simplified version of the rondo theme as the piano ornaments gently above. Soon this leads to a chuckling from the piano and winds, another cadenza, and the third and last appearance of the rondo theme. Beethoven modulates through several keys as he approaches the long coda. A cadenza based on a number of the themes opens with fire but soon turns lyrical, and the soothing winds dominate the orchestra in the long, lovely falling sequence that follows. But trills and an exciting speed-up lead to the dashing closing paragraph of Beethoven's most interesting and personal piano concerto.

No one would describe Beethoven's last piano concerto, the Fifth, as intimate. Mammoth in size, scope, and technical difficulty, this majestic composition of 1809 is the composer's best-known and most-loved work for piano and orchestra. The origin of the nickname is uncertain, but it was not Beethoven's. To many, the grandeur of the work justifies the nickname; others, including the nineteenth-century English historian George Grove, dismissed it,[2] while his countryman the great musicologist Donald Francis Tovey considered it vulgar and refused to use it.[3] For most musicians and listeners now, that name has been welded so tightly to the work that it stands as identification and little else.

The spaciousness and majesty of the Fifth Concerto is evident in all three movements: the opening Allegro, one of Beethoven's longest (582 measures, and typically taking just under twenty minutes to play), is without question an epic utterance. The hymnlike second movement is hypnotic in its shimmering, tranquil beauty, and the closing rondo, again one of Beethoven's largest essays in the form, is an immense and intoxicating dance. Enormous in scale, the "Emperor" Concerto also displays from start to finish an inner strength and serenity. The moments where real stresses are perceptible are few and seem more like masks picked up, then dropped as local events in the musical flow demand. The mood is different from that of, say, the "Appassionata" Sonata, where the drama is a genuine motivator of the tragic score. Unlike the quirky, highly personal idiom of the Fourth Concerto, the musical ideas in the Fifth are on glittering display throughout.

Beethoven begins the first movement with three immense chords, played *fortissimo* by the full orchestra, to each of which the piano replies with long, unfurling cadenzas of the utmost brilliance. No thematic material is presented here, but the first chord, E-flat major, defines the home key of the work, while the two that follow—A-flat major and B-flat major—are the home key's, and the movement's, two closely related secondary tonal centers. By opening with the piano fully engaged, Beethoven follows his own precedent established in the Fourth Piano Concerto. But the characters of the two openings have little in common, with this one flaunting its sonic splendor and athletic pianism. After the opening sequence, which takes well over a minute to play, the orchestra plays the main theme of the movement, proud and marchlike. When you listen, note the little turn followed at once by a soaring melodic motive that passes from the violins to the clarinets, then to the brass, and back to the violins in a higher pitch, both of which play major roles in the course of the movement. A second thematic element follows, an incisive tune in a short-short-long rhythm. And listen, too, to the unusual prominence Beethoven gives to the timpani, which emerge from their normal background role to a rare place in the sun, in both this movement and the finale.

The briefer second theme, in a curious flickering rhythm, covering little melodic ground and hovering unsurely between major and minor, is introduced by the strings, accompanied by clarinets and bassoons. Soon the horns and timpani enter, offering tonic stability and bringing on their heels the main theme. The full orchestra pursues a long discussion from which another important thematic idea emerges, a more even-tempered, lyrical tune in the form of falling scales. And finally, after more than four minutes of exposition, the piano reenters on a long, dainty scale, then presents the main theme in the tone of Olympian

calm that pervades the entire concerto. Soon, however, Beethoven asks
the player to perform acrobatics around a new incarnation of the incisive tune. Next comes a thoughtful presentation of the second theme,
which sounds dreamy, relaxed, and a bit mysterious in its new setting,
high on the keyboard.

The dreamy tone gives way to a presentation of the flickering second
theme in a new and strong and surprising march rhythm, though
Beethoven's tone in the passage seems jovial. Next, in a passage of great
power, the piano dissects the melodic turn of the opening over falling
triplets that hammer imperiously in the left hand. The suave lyrical
tune in falling scales dominates the texture as Beethoven prepares the
way for the return of the main theme to mark the start of the development. Here he gives new prominence to a tiny, simple three-note figure
in a march rhythm, which is integrated and developed to astonishing
degree, given its brevity. The development, which contains some very
beautiful dialogues for the piano and the winds, travels through some
faraway keys, creating effects that are mysterious but never threaten-
ing. Even the stormy passage where the solo instrument trades the little
march motive with the winds, brass, and timpani seems a sublime game
rather than a genuine battle; and the jogging contrapuntal exchange
that follows—note when you listen to the unmistakable humor in the
contribution of the bassoon—ends sweetly in a lyrical melody that made
its first appearance a bit earlier.

Beethoven brings back the turn in the original melody to pave
the way for the recapitulation, in which he first presents the opening
chords, now almost blindingly radiant and complete with somewhat
shorter cadenzas. Winds and piano comment at length and lyrically
on the main ideas, all of which pass once more in majestic procession.
Using the hammering of the three-note march motive interspersed with
grandiose scales that recall the three opening cadenzas, Beethoven paves
the way for the cadenza. At the big dominant chord that immediately
precedes the empty space in the score where performers would normally be expected to improvise a cadenza is a note: *NB. Non si fa una
Cadenza, ma s'attacca subito il seguente*: Don't make [*sic*] a cadenza, but
play the following immediately. Beethoven then writes out a cadenza-
like passage for the solo instrument that's powerful but considerably

shorter than a normal cadenza. It ends on the second theme, and before long the orchestra has quietly joined in. One reason Beethoven writes his own short cadenza rather than leaving it to the pianist is that the three mighty ones that open the work and are echoed later in the movement fill the role of the cadenza here and change the movement's proportions. And surely he also doubted the taste and discretion of players to interpolate a proper cadenza. By now we are well into the coda, which, like the movement it completes, is of titanic proportions—about one hundred bars. Note, when you listen, to the powerful rising figure of the piano's interjections and the huge figure for winds and strings that pushes the piano's part like a groundswell. The three-note march motive dominates to the glorious end.

The slow movement, based on a beautiful, hymnlike theme, is straightforward in construction but highly unusual in its key: B major, far from the E-flat major of the surrounding movements. But in its remoteness from the tonality that dominates the two massive outer movements lies its effectiveness, for it gives the piece a nocturnal effect between the bright daylight of its siblings. Beethoven amplifies the cool, silvery effect by muting the strings. His tempo marking, *adagio un poco mosso*—slowly flowing but a little quick—is also rare but makes it clear that the composer wanted it played with an easy but steady flow. The lush melodiousness and straightforward structure of the movement offer a moment of calm amid the heroic complexities of the first movement and the rondo.

The muted strings playing in their low registers chant the lovely and memorable main theme, richly harmonized, at the outset. Note when you listen how the tune rises to a high note in its third phrase, and the long, luxurious unwinding of the tune in its closing sequence. The entrance of the piano on moonlit descending triplets, playing a decorated variant of the melody, is also memorable and moving. A sequence of thirds for the piano leads to a chain of rising trills, then a beautifully ornamented rendering by the solo instrument of the main melody over easygoing triplets in the left hand and the plucked strings of the orchestra. This is the third instance in the concerto slow movements—the others are in the First and Third—where the piano soars ecstatically above strings playing pizzicato. The winds comment in sweet phrases above as the piano assumes the role of decorator to the orchestra's iteration of the main melody.

Beethoven gives the theme plenty of room to fall and fade in both pitch and volume. But instead of a firm close, the strings drop a quiet but thrilling half-step—a destabilizing and exciting move that signals the presentation of the rondo theme, slowly and in a magically embryonic form. Suddenly the piano plays the surging theme in unmistakable waltz rhythm as it leaps up, then falls. A second, complementary phrase only falls, but the complete tune is huge (fourteen measures) and surprisingly detailed and expressive beneath its jubilant posture. As in the Fourth Concerto, the movement has no contrasting episodes.

The solo piano presents an elegant new theme over a graceful left hand that makes for the start of an episode-like passage that is not, however, a genuine specimen. The second appearance of the rondo theme comes in the piano, accompanied by two horns holding a single B-flat and making rhythmic, almost percussive interjections. A mock-contrapuntal idea begins but peters out quickly, as does a mock-*furioso* phrase later in this long central section, where piano and orchestra trade thematic fragments and move from key to key in a passage that closely resembles a development. A long trill for the piano as the strings play quiet, compressed fragments of the main theme leads to the third presentation of the rondo theme, again by the solo piano and the horns. The full orchestra plays out the theme in a magnificent complete statement. Listen for the splendid contribution of the timpani here, which shadows a spinning melodic tail played in fast-moving sixteenth notes in the strings. The piano returns with fast scales, playing its elegant tune from earlier over a gentle string accompaniment, then moving high up the keyboard to render a glitteringly elaborated version of the theme.

The orchestra takes over for the fourth and last appearance of the rondo theme, which it presents in its ripest version, with strings decorating the long tune as presented by the rest of the instruments. The piano makes playful comments along the way. Finally, the piano begins the remarkable coda with the same scale figure with which it made two swaggering entrances earlier. But its improbable companion here is the timpani, and the two instruments engage in a witty dialogue, in which the timpani taps out the dance rhythm (*long*-short-long-long-

long-long) on which the entire movement is based while the solo piano plays a lyrical dying fall. (No question that Bartók, composer of the Sonata for Two Pianos and Percussion, knew this wonderful page!) But the scales race ahead once more, and the full orchestra ends the work with the memorable leaping figure that forms the strongest part of the first theme's profile. Thus, Beethoven maintains his powerful structural grip all the way to the final notes of this vast rondo movement.

The Earliest Sonatas

Opp. 2, 7, 10, and 13, the "Pathétique"

Beethoven published his first three piano sonatas in 1796, dedicating them to Haydn. Composed a year earlier, these are fine, fiery works by the young master, adored by most listeners who know them and in no way light, inferior, or juvenile. They speak a classical sonata language that Beethoven at the age of twenty-five had already made his own. By the time he reached thirty and had written the last sonatas covered in this chapter, he had mastered the style. He went on to transform it utterly.

The Sonata No. 1 is in F minor, an unusual key in 1796 for such a large-scale work. Although its keyboard textures are lighter than those of its companion works in Op. 2, it is an unusually dark, serious piece, sleekly built and consistent in tone from start to finish. It seems fitting that the series begin with this gem, which combines the composer's already formidable structural sense with a fresh, youthful passion. Lack of space unfortunately prevents the inclusion of the entire sonata on the CD included with this book, but the splendid last movement is the second track.

The first movement opens with a rising melodic phrase that is identical with that of the finale of Mozart's G Minor Symphony, K. 550; this type of subject, consisting of the tonic chord (here, of course, F minor) broken into rising detached notes, was known as a "Mannheim rocket," after the composers centered in Mannheim, Germany (Karl Stamitz is the best-known of them), who devised it. Its sound in these two examples is of an unyielding firmness, crisply expressed. The second theme differs from the opening in most possible ways, being in A-flat major, rhythmically unstable, legato (connected) rather than detached, and agitated rather than firm. Beethoven plays the two off against each other in the development, making much of a little turn at the top of the opening tune and ending the movement quite magnificently on the phrase that ended the exposition, followed by big chords interspersed with dramatic silences and an avalanche of angry chords at the very end.

The second movement is in aria form, meaning that it's an instrumental version of an operatic aria. Mozart used it often in his sonatas and concertos, and Beethoven follows that form here without sounding a bit like Mozart. The movement opens with a slow, songful melody stated directly at the beginning, then reiterated in a minor key. The composer brings the original tune back, decorates it more heavily, and then restates it over a flowing, broken-chord accompaniment known as an Alberti bass. In its final appearance, the melody almost seems to dissolve in ornamentation.

The stern Beethoven we know well appears in the menuetto, in which the hovering phrases of the opening contrast with the more flowing, grounded phrases that follow; the trio (the middle section) opens mildly in F major but soon ends on a more emphatic, agitated phrase in a thicker texture.

The finale (CD Track 2) is great example of Beethoven's stormy early style and his willingness to tinker with and stretch form. It's in sonata form, to demonstrate that the movement is serious, but Beethoven modifies its structure by adding a lyrical episode to the development section. Carrying the unusual tempo marking *prestissimo*—very quickly—a headlong rushing of triplets in the left hand under a barrage of angry chords in the right stated right at the opening marks the memorable first subject. The moaning theme in falling quarter notes in the left hand at 0:25 is the second subject, and the first returns at 0:58 to round out the exposition, which is repeated at 1:05–2:10. Starting the development with a modified version of the crashing chords of the opening, Beethoven then introduces a long, lyrical episode based on two related melodies, the first appearing at 2:13 and the second at 2:36. At 3:10 Beethoven picks up the pattern of a traditional development, trading and blending thematic fragments until 3:44, when the recapitulation begins unmistakably. As is typical, the opening material is expanded and elaborated, as in, for example, the elegant descending embroidery for the right hand beginning at 3:54. And the fierce final passage, beginning at 4:43, is a whirlwind of virtuosic excitement and drama.

Although rarely performed outside complete surveys of the sonatas, No. 2 in A Major is remarkably bold and deserves broader interest than it gets. In the opening movement of this large-scale four-movement work Beethoven combines falling and rising mottoes—they're not really melodies—to form the first thematic group. The second theme is a daring conception with which the composer casts far into the musical future as it darts with rapid, nervous movements into remote keys, ending abruptly with a falling figure from the opening sequence that's apparently comic, but with a violent undertone. He rounds out the opening group with a broader, more jovial figure that also rises and falls, this time in broken octaves. The agitated development, which is highly contrapuntal in spots, involves close combinations and recombinations of thematic DNA. As in the opening section, however, Beethoven treats his material in radical ways for the era. The recapitulation includes a lovely, thoughtful postscript to the rising portion of the opening theme, and Beethoven ends this forward-looking movement quietly.

The slow movement is also highly unusual. Beethoven calls it a Largo appassionato—broadly and passionately. It consists of a long, arialike melody in the right hand, which he indicates is to be played in long-held notes against staccato notes in the left hand, presumably in imitation of strings playing pizzicato. But soon he breaks this for a more flowing, pianistic mode, in which the melody moves more conventionally. In the middle of this strange, complex movement, the keyboard writing is as thick as it has ever been up to that time, with a massive, nine-note chord in bar 31, for example. The harmony turns briefly and dramatically to the minor as the opening theme returns, and in the very long coda Beethoven adds another hesitant decorative line into the mix. This long movement, somewhat peculiar in its structure, sonority, keyboard textures, and themes, testifies to the young Beethoven's ambition and willingness to experiment.

The brief scherzo is probably the most conventional movement of the four, but here, too, Beethoven plays in a rather Haydnesque way with

bits of phrases and rhythm so that the listener's ear is tickled—charmingly in this case—by their instability. Beethoven lengthens phrases
beautifully in the trio.

Beethoven pulls out another unusual expression mark for the closing
rondo: *grazioso*, or graceful. But this, too, seems more than a little misleading, as agitation seems to underlie much of this interesting movement. The principal theme opens with a long arpeggio that Beethoven
extends and makes more emphatic on each of its several returns. An
enormous drop of thirteen notes leads to the central melodic phrase,
which is graceful indeed. The temporizing second theme is also long and
a bit nervous. The long, contrasting middle section in A minor sounds
emphatic and a bit militaristic in its rage (whether genuine or mock,
the latter seeming more likely). But Beethoven finally settles down
and returns to the opening rondo material, weaving between keys and
finally coming to rest on a quiet, elegant cadence.

Beethoven rounds out Op. 2 with a big, four-movement work in C
major that's completely different in character from its fellows. In this
big-boned, virtuoso showpiece the composer displays a proud, extroverted mastery of keyboard and musical styles. The problem with most
recorded performances is that its thick textures and aggressive nature
often come off sounding like breaking crockery on a modern piano.
The lighter tone of the composer's instrument, built around 1800,
would have clarified these passages. As it is, even distinguished players
regularly lose control at the same predictable points in the score: they
may hit all the notes, but they also bang and make other ugly sounds.
One notable exception is the great English pianist Solomon, whose 1951
performance, reissued in 2000, displays the austere control and refined
musicianship the modern keyboard requires for this work.

The first movement opens quietly with a marvelous, wiggly figure
that's reputedly hard to execute; then, for twelve measures Beethoven
keeps the volume low and textures to a demure four parts. But then the
music erupts in a furious *fortissimo* barrage of pure keyboard writing,
arpeggios and broken tenths (an unusually wide stretch to play) over
fierce, drumming rhythmic figures. (This is one of the passages that
generally gets away from pianists.) A busy Mozartean figure rounds out
the first subject. The second subject begins with a lovely, lyrical idea

in G minor that gives way to an aggressive figure but then melts into another gorgeous phrase, this one in C major. The big *fortissimo* salvo returns, followed by several new ideas, all pithy but punchy, and a final, thunderous scale that rises and falls in broken octaves.

A wild, cadenza-like passage in a rainbow of keys is perhaps the most interesting feature of the development. It's later echoed in the expanded recapitulation section in a long fantasia-like passage that leads to a genuine, miniature cadenza—the showy solo passage in a concerto—based on the opening subject, even though this is of course a work for a solo instrument. But it further emphasizes the extroverted, masculine nature of this movement, where in all instances Beethoven reaches for what is bigger and bolder, as does the fiercely athletic coda, ending in the racing scale in broken octaves.

The beautiful Adagio is perhaps the high point of the work. It's unusual for its key of E major—far from the norm for a high-classical work in C major—and also as for its clear structure. Charles Rosen observes that the opening melody "has an operatic cast . . . [with] a pause in every bar, as if the singer stopped for breath after each brief motif: every silence, as in an opera, has an emotional power."[1] The remainder of the movement consists of alternations of the opening theme with a beautiful flowing idea that roams freely through several new keys and involves constant hand crossing. In the middle of the movement Beethoven restates the opening theme without preparation and *fortissimo* in C major, which now sounds distant in the context of the keys in which we have been wandering. And the closing phrase is a rather striking musical gesture in which the composer moves the voices and hands in interesting and unexpected ways.

A catchy sparkle characterizes the scherzo, which, once heard, is easily remembered. The middle section consists of broad, rumbling arpeggios, and Beethoven adds an imaginative coda in which the energy of the movement seems to sputter out as we listen. The rondo-form finale is another large-scale movement, like the first, opening with a scampering theme clad in full pianistic regalia. A more suave theme follows, then a chorale. (The latter idea is one Brahms would appropriate for the last movement of his big Sonata No. 3 in F Minor.) While this movement is manifestly virtuosic, it's lighter in touch and more graceful in spirit than the thunderous opening section. Still, the difficulties it presents the player are formidable.

Beethoven composed the fourth sonata, the Sonata in E-flat Major, in 1796; it was published as Op. 7 the following year. This long, technically difficult, highly polished work represents a major step forward in and expansion of the form in which the composer stretches all the boundaries he set in Op. 2, but with a lyrical suavity. Like its predecessors, Op. 7 is rarely performed outside complete surveys of the series.

The first movement overflows with ideas. The opening throbs with excitement as a long-short chord sequence in the right hand calls out over the steady pulse of individual notes in the left. A more lyrical melodic group follows, then a playful transitional one; after that we hear the second thematic group, which opens with a more complex, rhythmically sophisticated theme. Next follows a sort of chorale, similar to the one in the last movement of Op. 2 No. 3. All of this comes at the listener at brisk speed and with considerable mechanical difficulties for the player. The last and most difficult idea of the opening group to execute is a figure in shuddering sixteenth notes, which the right hand plays over long-held notes in the left. The movement is also a remarkable exploration of the many faces of the compound 6/8 meter, from lilting, to soothing, racing, leaping, and more. And throughout the movement, Beethoven's long phrases create a sense of a continually unrolling spaciousness and grandeur.

The majestic, three-part slow movement carries the tempo and expression mark Largo, con gran espressione—broadly, with great expression. The opening tune is long-breathed—twenty-four measures—and includes a number of pauses as it grandly rises and falls. The middle section features a new melody over staccato sixteenth notes, then a curious, unaccompanied chirping phrase in the right hand. A long, expressive coda ends this noble utterance. The scherzo that follows, labeled Allegro, also contains many pauses built into its main theme, but the affect is more hesitant and wistful here than in the preceding Largo. But the feeling is playful, too, and the music maintains its relatively consistent suavity. Beethoven builds the surging trio—another very difficult passage to play—from a sequence of triplets from which the E-flat minor melody rises in ghostly fashion.

The composer carries the gentle, hesitant tone of the scherzo—not really typical for him—into the big rondo that ends this spectacular work. The difficult-to-translate tempo marking is all moderation, and the composer builds delicious hesitations and delays into the main theme. The first episode is playful, the second mock-stormy, and both vanish in a wave of Beethoven's hand. But he saves his real magic for the end, in a quiet but astonishing passage, where with utmost daring he twists the harmony to the remote key of E major, then finds his way back to end the movement quietly and ecstatically in E-flat major.

Beethoven composed the three sonatas that make up the Op. 10 set in 1797; they were published the following year. They are remarkable for their diversity and for the sense they give that the composer is pushing forcefully ahead with his experiments of style. The first two works are both in three movements and highly compressed, while the third is an expansive piece in four movements, similar in dimension to the Opp. 2 and 7 sonatas, as well as to the larger-scale sonatas to come.

The first sonata of Op. 10 is also the first of Beethoven's three sonatas in C minor, perhaps the best-known and most characteristic key in which he wrote. The other two are the famous "Pathétique" of the following year and the otherworldly Op. 111 of 1823; other important C minor works include the Piano Concerto No. 3 and, of course, the Symphony No. 5. Unfortunately, Op. 10 No. 1 is played far less often than its sonata cousins in C minor, but it's a splendid piece, too.

The opening movement consists of contrasts between the first thematic group, based on a broken C minor chord that storms upward in a jagged rhythm and a long-spun melody over a fleet, rocking accompaniment. Beethoven wastes no time on rhetorical gestures in the development, where the second theme is heard in a wailing mode, the momentum kept going by means of subtle rhythmic devices.

In the middle movement, marked *Adagio molto*, Beethoven subjects an opulent, arialike theme to elaborate decorative treatment. The melody's simplicity recalls some of Mozart's opera arias, while the elaborate ornamentation looks ahead to the expressivity of Bellini's style on the operatic stage and Chopin's at the keyboard. This, the longest movement by far of the sonata, is its calm centerpiece, where long phrases contrast with the far more urgent expression of the flanking movements. Beethoven places a dramatic chord at its center, then repeats the melody with new decorations, adding a long coda and some lovely dying fall effects.

Taut and tense, the finale is not a rondo, but a stripped-down, high-speed essay in sonata form. It's significant that the composer chose a conflict-laden structure for the driven closing section. The mood is all breathless urgency except for one held-back passage just before the muttered end, after which Beethoven switches melodramatically to C major, increasing tension rather than creating the peaceful resolution that tonic minor to major shifts usually mean.

While the F Major Sonata, Op. 10 No. 2, shares a compactness with its C minor companion work, its humorous tone is entirely different. According to Tovey,[2] Beethoven retained an affection for this quirky piece for years. Certainly one can hear echoes of its density and wit in some later works in the same key, notably the strange and singular Sonata Op. 54.

This mostly droll work, without doubt neglected among its more showy peers, opens with a movement of musical epigrams. The opening subject is a motto rather than a melody, followed by another, more fluid idea that is, however, still rather tongue-tied; then the second subject arches in the right hand over a galumphing accompaniment in the left. There are some new ideas, expressed with a vehemence that comically exceeds their significance, emphatic pauses, and a closing phrase featuring burbling trills in which the bliss seems genuine. The composer makes much ado about nothing in the development, where he breaks figurations apart into hilariously isolated phrases, sometimes mincing, sometimes manic.

Beethoven saw that a deep or placid Adagio would be out of place in this short composition. So instead he changes the pace and mood in the second movement, substituting a flowing minuet of veiled melancholy in F minor with a central Trio. A particularly haunting moment comes with the return of the first theme, where Beethoven breaks its rhythm delicately in the right hand over the accompaniment in the left. This strategy has several descendants in Beethoven's oeuvre, the first of which, as we shall soon see, is the second movement of the E Major Sonata, Op. 14 No. 1, another swaying dance in the tonic minor key.

The composer returns to comedy for the finale, a headlong rush, in unserious fugal style, of unflagging rhythmic drive. At first, Beethoven seems Teutonically earnest in his need to pursue part writing; then, halfway through the course, he turns the movement into to an elfin dance. The ending is hammered home abruptly, in octaves. The finale is far more difficult to play than first two movements.

Cut from a different cloth from its intriguing companions in Op. 10, the third and last sonata of the set is a grandly scaled four-movement work. The first part begins directly with a memorable, energetic, scale-based theme that's not exactly tuneful but is still too long to be called a motto. Beethoven follows it with clearer melodies in minor keys that, despite their darker tonalities, set off the opening phrase to handsome effect. The second theme is a typical classical "feminine" complement to the forceful opening, a graceful falling theme in a weaker rhythm. Many other ideas follow, and Beethoven ends the whole group with a chorale-like figure. With so much material in the exposition, the development is long as well, but it flies by at Beethoven's *presto* tempo. There is also an action-packed coda.

The slow movement is surely the greatest Beethoven had written for the keyboard up to this time, and one of his most beautiful and moving from any period, early, middle, or late. His tempo and expression mark, *Largo e mesto*—broad and sad, or troubled—is unusual and worth noting. This sonata-form movement is an important example of the "pathetic" style in Beethoven's early work. The word had a different meaning in the early nineteenth century: to Beethoven and his contemporaries, the term "pathetic" indicated pathos, or passion, and high emotion.

The opening theme curls tragically on itself over heavy chords in the left hand before moving into more fluid phrasing, then a clear, "pathetic" melody in the right over a broken-chord accompaniment in the left. Again, Beethoven thickens the keyboard textures into rich chords, but dense keyboard writing is typical of certain passages here. A theme that resembles a tragic recitative or dialogue follows, then a remarkable phrase resembling sighing or weeping—at first high on the keyboard, then a descent interrupted by long, devastated pauses. After the recapitulation of the main theme comes a remarkable, gripping coda, in which the right hand breaks into long arpeggios over the theme stretched into a different rhythm in the left hand—the lower notes. Some funereal chords, a few sighs, and two notes deep in the bass end this grand, youthful expression of Beethoven's ripening tragic vision.

Beethoven makes a graceful transition from the dark slow movement to the minuet. Its gentle themes, presented in a sequence of marvelously balanced phrases, are offset by a trio that's rougher in character, with a two-note phrase for a rapidly crossing left hand set against fast triplets in the right. The finale is a curious rondo that is not without problems for the interpreter. It sets a hesitant three-note phrase against long pauses, some humorous passages, stark dynamic contrasts, and a harmonically unmoored phrase that looks ahead to Debussy. A gentle series of syncopated (off-the-beat) chords modulates to the final fade-down, which sets the three-note figure against a long scale. Quietly rippling figuration brings the work to a calm conclusion.

Once so inescapable in recital and the teacher's studio that it threatened to become hackneyed, the Sonata No. 8 in C Minor, the "Pathétique," has fallen from the heights of popularity and is now heard less frequently. That it may have been overexposed for generations never detracted from its inherent splendor. The wonder its early audiences felt at its daring naturally diminished as years passed, as Beethoven pushed the frontiers of his own style and was followed in turn by other great composers who wrote countless bold works in new styles. But in Beethoven's lifetime the "Pathétique" was one of the works that distinguished him as an original and profound musical thinker. A memoir by the pianist-composer Ignaz Moscheles (1794–1870), once renowned and now nearly forgotten, helps to give a sense of the novelty and power of this music:

> To satisfy my curiosity about this so-called eccentric genius there I
> found a copy of his "Sonata pathétique.". . . The style was so novel,
> and I became so excited by it that in my admiration I forgot to
> tell my teacher. When I did he warned me off such eccentric pro-
> ductions until I had based my style upon more solid models. . . . I
> ignored him and seized upon the pianoforte works of Beethoven
> as they appeared, and in them found a solace and a delight such as
> no composer delighted [or] afforded me.[3]

Beethoven himself seems, for once, to have bestowed the nickname on this work, which was published in 1799 and probably composed the year before. As noted, another close-to-hand example of a work in the pathetic mode by Beethoven would be the Largo e mesto—the big, tragic slow movement—of the previous sonata, the D Major, Op. 10 No. 3. In the remarkable work now under examination, Beethoven reaches for the grandest style available to him at this early stage of his career. The "Pathétique" Sonata represents the spectacular culmination of his earliest efforts in the field of the piano sonata.

The opening movement is large in dimension and bold in structure. Beethoven begins with a shattering passage, modeled on the old form of the French overture. Used as operatic overtures or as opening movements to instrumental suites by Bach, Handel, and other composers of the baroque era, these are stately compositions with opening passages in slow tempo and dotted (an exaggerated long-short) rhythm that eventually give way to a more flowing, cheerful section. But here, Beethoven sits so heavily on his thick chords that the mood he establishes is unmistakably tragic. These chords alternate with stark, stalking phrases, then with more flowing passagework as the composer prepares the way for the main body of this sonata movement, but the darkness cast by the introduction looms over the entire first movement. And that's not the only way Beethoven makes sure the somber mood holds: in a bold formal move, he twice reintroduces the slow introduction into the body of the movement, a procedure that was exceedingly rare, if not absolutely novel, when he did it.

A choppy theme rises, then falls in detached notes over a *tremolando* in the left hand to form the agitated first subject. The second subject is a more contained and somber but still swiftly flowing melody, characterized by some elegant little trills known as mordents. Both subjects, unusually, are in minor keys—the first, C minor, and the second, E-flat minor. A classical sonata with a first subject in a minor key will more typically present the second subject in a contrasting, major tonality, so Beethoven's insistence on minor keys here is worth noticing for its unrelenting seriousness. This gives way to an agitated, surging phrase, at last in E-flat major, that will figure prominently in the development section. Beethoven repeats the exposition, but on its second return, he reintroduces a shortened version of the introduction, stopping the furious momentum cold once more. Again, this may seem relatively mild to listeners today, but it was wildly dramatic and daring to Beethoven's audience around 1800.

The development is notable for a climactic passage wherein the composer sets double trills in the right hand far above syncopated notes thundering far below in the left. It's based on the surging E-flat major passage from late in the exposition, but here Beethoven makes it boil. This striking effect, of very high and low notes sounded together, is one that fascinated Beethoven and to which he returned throughout his entire career as a composer for the piano.

Once again, just when we think Beethoven is guiding the movement toward its logical and emotional conclusion, he surprises us by once more interjecting four bars of the slow, heavy, powerful introductory material, though played softly this time; he then closes this astonishing movement with the rushing main subject followed by four biting chords.

The slow movement, based on a lush tune modeled lovingly in the style of Italian arias, is one of Beethoven's most famous. The grand, arching main melody is so memorable and heart-easing that it readily embeds itself in most listeners' memories. (There's a good chance you've heard it already.) Formally, the movement is a rondo with two episodes, the first in the style of a recitative for two voices, the second a more dramatic, harmonically adventurous passage above which the main theme floats in a more troubled incarnation. The final appearance of the main theme comes over a throbbing triplet accompaniment, and Beethoven rounds this reposeful movement off with a short, graceful coda.

Beethoven does not attempt to recapture the power and drama of the opening movement in the closing rondo. But its tight, elegantly cut design, with a welcome bit of humor, provides a marvelous conclusion to the "Pathétique" Sonata. The main theme is serious but lilting, marked by grace notes; the first episode is dense with ideas, each of which is brief but full of character. The second episode is notable for a contrapuntal passage, where Beethoven works in mock solemnity in two voices, then three, before playfully moving on. And, as in the first movement, the coda is striking: first Beethoven builds intensity with triplets over thick chords, then pauses after a long, fierce scale. He states the theme twice, richly, in A-flat major, then brings this musical landmark to an end on a savage downward scale.

Early-Middle Masterworks
Sonatas 9–15

The sonatas we'll look at in this chapter form a remarkably varied group, all composed by Beethoven in the fertile years between about 1799 and 1802. They include several undeservedly neglected pieces—the two shorter works of Op. 14 and the more ambitious Op. 22, for example—as well as the most popular of all Beethoven's piano sonatas, the "Moonlight," Op. 27 No. 2. While these are generally classified as members of the composer's early period, a listener who studies them in order will hear a progression and expansion in size and complexity as they go from the delicate Op. 14 pair to the very considerable dimensions of Op. 28, a long and complex work of 1801 that also gives a clear sense of the larger works soon to come. And, despite Beethoven's increasing deafness, these energetic pieces generally continue in the upbeat mood of the works that preceded them—with one notable exception, the "Moonlight."

The two short works of Op. 14 are believed to date to 1799, the year they were published. Both are modest in dimension and, apart from the "easy" Op. 49 sonatas, the most straightforward of the series technically, though still not for beginners. Seldom heard in the concert hall, especially No. 2, their obscurity and lack of pretension mustn't keep you from getting the most from this deliciously lyrical pair.

Note, when you listen to the opening phrase of the Sonata No. 9 in E Major, Op. 14 No. 1, to the relaxed, conversational quality of the material. Beethoven presents his material in sonata form with the tone that of a civilized discussion rather than a conflict or drama. Some thick keyboard textures and brusque phrases, however, are utterly Beethovenian; they could come from the pen of no other composer.

The development presents a new, long-limbed, lyrical melody over an urgent arpeggiated accompaniment. Beethoven winds the movement down quietly over some grumbling chord sequences in the left hand. The slow movement is a descendant of its cousin from Op. 10 No. 2, a lyrical minuet in the tonic minor (in this case E minor). The haunting melody, all shadows and sighs, stays in the listener's memory with ease. As has been pointed out,[1] the moderate tempo of the minuet fills the role of both slow movement and minuet or scherzo in this relatively brief work. In the short rondo, Beethoven puts his breathless theme through its paces against a racing episode in triplets before bringing it back in a comically stuttering, syncopated form.

The Sonata No. 10 in G Major, Op. 14 No. 2, is a neglected little gem that offers many pleasures. The opening theme is a penetrating melody of a type we have not encountered in the sonatas before: articulate without rhetoric, poised between music and speech, reminiscent of birdsong. The second theme is an arching tune in thirds, and Beethoven rounds out the exposition with a closing theme of infinite tenderness that sounds like an operatic trio as a melodic thread from the left hand joins in, like a bass singing his part. Beethoven redistributes this delicate material in the swift development section, itself split into two parts, subjecting the first theme to a hail of triplets and minor-key alterations, as well giving it to the left hand. The opening material returns in expanded form, and Beethoven ends this exquisite movement on a poetically phrased musical question.

For the second movement, the composer presents a comically simple theme and three variations. It's an exercise after the manner of Haydn, its apparent simplicity masking considerable sophistication of harmony and rhythm. But these variations display Beethoven's more aggressive nature, with sharply accented syncopations and thicker, heavier chords than his teacher typically employed. Like Haydn, he saves a big surprise for the end, as he moves listeners along dreamily toward a final cadence in dainty little chords played softly, then springs the trap with a big, full, *fortissimo* closing.

Beethoven's telling title for the rondo that closes the sonata is Scherzo, presumably to highlight its playful character. The springy main theme is interrupted by three episodes, two of which are comic, one lyric, but the sense of forward motion is constant and breathtaking. The composer keeps his textures light, ending this brilliant movement on a witty grumble deep in the keyboard.

Beethoven expressed pride in his Sonata No. 11 in B-flat Major, Op. 22.[2] But the work is one of the least popular of the series, with the fewest recordings on the market of any but the little Op. 49 No. 1. The opinionated pianist Glenn Gould even called Op. 22 "a dud."[3] And indeed, some of its material has a somewhat formulaic cast, and the structures of this four-movement work composed in 1799–1800 look backward to the more conservative aspects of its cousins of Opp. 2 and 7 and Op. 10 No. 3. Throughout the old-fashioned four-movement format of Op. 22—with its sonata-form opening movement, arialike Adagio, Menuetto, and Rondo—Beethoven seems focused chiefly on craftsmanship and structure. But it would be a mistake to ignore the intellectual pleasures this superb and spirited work offers; take Gould's comment or leave it and make up your own mind.

The brisk first movement opens with a wiggling figure in the right hand over a bump in the bass that together form a broken B-flat major chord, followed by a series of similarly energetic themes that make up the first theme group. As is typical for a high-classical sonata-form movement, the second subject is easier in rhythm, though not particularly "feminine" in the usual manner of second subjects. But the most important element of the exposition to listen for is the closing theme, hammered out in forceful octaves that rise, then fall, followed by the wiggle of the opening figure and two strong cadential chords.

The passage that elicits the admiration of critics and connoisseurs comes in the development section. Beethoven makes the forceful closing theme of the exposition the primary topic of this closely argued passage, placing it deep in the bass, repeating it again and again beneath a stream of arpeggios expressing a dark, shifting (minor ninth) harmony. Beethoven extends the recapitulation by just a few notes, then ends the movement, in true eighteenth-century style, without a coda.

In the long and beautiful slow movement, Beethoven adapts the lavishly decorated melody of a slow, lyrical Italian opera aria for the piano. The right-hand melody is a beautifully sculpted, convincing adaptation for the piano of the Italian vocal style, with stepwise legato notes typical of the style, dramatic pauses, turns, runs, and drooping phrases. Beethoven keeps the accompaniment for the most part to quietly puls- ing chords in the left hand. A murmuring passage in the development section (the movement is in sonata form) is lovely and effective.

Mozart wrote countless aria take-offs as slow movements for his instrumental works, bringing them off effortlessly in his lighter-tex- tured style. And although Chopin has been disparaged as a "composer for the right hand," he took these idealized arias for the piano to their highest peak. It's fair to point out, without denigrating Beethoven or this wonderful movement, that Chopin's left-hand accompaniments in his nocturnes and other works with melodies similar to those here are always far more inventive and expressive than Beethoven's plain chordal accompaniment. This movement is a good example of Beethoven's occasional indifference to the sound and potential of his instrument, and even to the best way of setting his ideas. But Beethoven went on to develop his skill at writing left-hand accompaniments to operatically styled melodies, culminating in the sublime slow movement of the "Hammerklavier" Sonata (discussed in chapter 9.)

The Minuet seems to be the last in the sonatas in the old style, built on a lilting, easygoing melody. But some of the passages that follow express greater agitation, and the Trio, in G minor, has real bite. The tightly organized and substantial Rondo opens on a mild-mannered sub- ject with an eighteenth-century feel. But Beethoven has some tricks up his sleeve. One is a little transitional passage of running notes, subjected to continual rhythmic compression that teases the listeners' ears. More significant is the second episode, stern in character and contrapuntal in feeling, which he brings back for extensive development later; mate- rial from rondo episodes does not typically recur (see pp. 10–11). The composer uses the stern theme a third time, now more playfully in the major key, to introduce the fine coda.

Form and content blend happily in the beautiful Sonata No. 12 in A-flat Major, Op. 26. In this striking work from 1800, Beethoven gives unusual forms to two of the four movements: the first is a set of variations on a lyrical theme, and the third, a funeral march. The second and fourth movements are a scherzo and a rondo, but these, too, have such strong profiles that all four sections might be considered character pieces. Tovey states that the ancestry of this singular work is the divertimento, a relaxed, multi-movement instrumental form of the classical era, of which Haydn and Mozart wrote many, rather than the more intense, contrapuntally driven partita or suite of the baroque era.[4] Among Mozart's piano sonatas, the three-movement K. 331, in A major, is another likely forerunner, as it also opens with a variation movement that's longer and showier than Beethoven's in Op. 26 and is followed by a grand minuet. Mozart ends his sonata with a famous Rondo alla turca. It's a great work that Beethoven must have studied. Finally, Op. 26 was the Beethoven sonata that Chopin taught and played more than any other.[5] Coincidentally or not, the Polish master's turbulent Sonata No. 2 contains the most famous of all funeral marches; but unlike Op. 26, Chopin's sonata was first perceived as a collection of disparate movements, its inner unity revealing itself only gradually. (Another fantasy for music lovers is to imagine hearing Chopin play Beethoven's Op. 26.)

Beethoven opens the work with a variation movement in a very moderate tempo. The three-part theme is warm, memorable, rhythmically fairly simple, and richly harmonized, a typical and tasty example of the kind of theme Haydn, Mozart, Beethoven, and Schubert used for their variations. Note when you listen to the little turn in the fourth measure, a musical fingerprint that turns up in all of the five variations that follow. The middle section has a more plaintive, questioning quality, to which the third part of the theme, which is essentially a reprise of the opening phrase, replies. The theme is also similar in profile and feeling to that of the *Six Variations on an Original Theme*, Op. 34, a marvelous work of two years later (see pp. 144–145).

In the first variation, Beethoven breaks the theme into arpeggios (broken chords) in the same rhythm as the melodic turn in the left hand, then ornaments the melody in the right in the second half of the section. The second variation places the melody into short notes in the left hand, harmonized by the right, in rapidly alternating notes. Imagine it as though you were watching something with a strobe light flashing, but the effect is more continuous and lyrical. Beethoven moves to the unusual key of A-flat minor for the third variation. The mood is altogether darker as he breaks the melody over its throbbing accompaniment. The composer takes us back to the major key in the fourth variation, which is rhythmically squeezed and a bit humorous. Lilting triplets dominate the rhythm of the lovely fifth variation, where Beethoven also speeds up his note values, anticipating the same technique in the final variation of the Op. 109 sonata, twenty years later (see p. 122). In both the feeling is of breaking loose, but Beethoven has a surprise in store in Op. 26: he appends a fifteen-bar coda where he introduces a fervent new melody, similar in spirit to the main theme, with which he seems to comment on the parade of beauty that just passed.

Driving rhythms dominates the scherzo, presenting an immense contrast with the lyric meditations of the opening movement. In its opening part, Beethoven sets a scampering theme to a variety of accents, some sharp, others more delicate, before finally taking off in a racing phrase; the trio has a steadier, rocking motion. But as is typical for this metrically complex passage, the composer highlights the transition back to the opening passage with exciting, sharply syncopated octaves in the right hand against the main theme as it rises in the left.

"Marcia funebre sulla morte d'un eroe"—Funeral March on the Death of a Hero—is Beethoven's title for the third movement, making it an example of program music, which is music that tells a story; of course, it anticipates the titanic funeral march Beethoven would write for the second movement of the Symphony No. 3, the "Eroica," of 1803. *Maestoso andante* is his tempo and expression mark; it means a stately walking pace. Most of the pianists who have recorded Op. 26 have obeyed the composer's instruction, moving at true march pace, not trying to slow down for false dramatic effect; the movement works much better at a genuine march tempo. Next to the high tragedy of either the "Eroica" march or Chopin's, this movement's affect is more cool and straight. The opening theme is a plain, nearly tuneless march, like one played by a military band, and in the middle section, the composer creates a remarkable imitation of drums and cannon. Beethoven brings back the opening passage, then winds the movement down in a quiet coda.

The fantastical finale is a rondo with two episodes that is also an essay in perpetual motion. Beethoven varies the gentle sound of the falling notes of the opening idea by inverting it, making them rise. As is typical, the material of both episodes contrasts with the main theme, but the unending stream of sixteenth notes carries the movement with its homogeneous texture and sound; Beethoven ends on a magical drop-off, low on the keyboard.

Beethoven gave both of the sonatas of Op. 27, which he published in 1802, the significant title *Sonata quasi una Fantasia*: in the style of a fantasia. This was a composition not entirely free in form but emotionally wide ranging, juxtaposing passages of radically different moods and written in a virtuosic keyboard style. There's no finer example of a high-classical keyboard fantasia than Mozart's K. 475, in C minor, which serves as a preface to the sonata in the same key, K. 457. With Op. 27 Beethoven signals to his audience of 1802 and the ages that followed that these two brave works are experiments in form.

Neither work is as free in form as the Mozart, but both push hard at the definition of what makes a sonata. Throughout No. 1 and between the first two movements of No. 2 Beethoven instructs the pianist to play the movements without breaks, yet each of these seven movements can stand on its own. In the E-flat major sonata, the composer anticipates Opp. 101 and 110, where he unexpectedly reprises material heard earlier in the finale to powerful effect. That Op. 27 No. 1 languishes in relative obscurity is probably due to the density of its material and the composer's greater intellectual focus relative to the second, in C-sharp minor—the "Moonlight"—which is by turns meditative, melancholy, passionate, and tragic, and with a sweep that makes it easier to appreciate. The "Moonlight" is Beethoven's most famous piano sonata—or at least it was; in recent decades the "Appassionata," Op. 57, appears to have overtaken it in popularity.

But a first-time listener to Op. 27 No. 1 will be forgiven for being puzzled by the opening of the work, which is comically bland. Beethoven sets the right hand to playing two quiet chords in the simplest harmonic sequence over a cello-like figure in the left. He dials up the intensity very slightly over the measures that follow, but when the music pauses and the middle section of the movement breaks in—a rough and fast German dance in C major—we wake up. Although the interruption is only seconds long, the whole composition now presents a more vigorous affect. The opening sequence returns; Beethoven ends the movement on a coda made of a condensed version of the initial idea.

Beethoven's instruction to the performer at the end of the first movement is *Attacca subito l'Allegro*—play the allegro immediately, don't pause between movements. The C minor scherzo places us squarely into Beethoven's second-period style. Aggressive and frightening, the melody, such as it is, emerges from broken-chord figuration that sweeps rapidly up and down the keyboard. Beethoven shifts to A-flat major for the trio, a ride in a thumping iambic (short-long) rhythm, with a snarling trill at its apex that some perceive as comic, others, nightmarish. Beethoven brings back the main section in syncopated form, and again the composer tells the player to proceed to the next movement, the Adagio, without pause.

Conceived in the operatic style of the Op. 22 slow movement, this melody emerges as a rapt, long-breathed utterance over a pulsing accompaniment, even though the tune is repeated. Here the left- and right-hand parts seem more skillfully interwoven, and the music casts a spell. The Adagio is brief, with scales, runs, and trills leading without pause, again, to the finale, which is the longest and most complex movement in the sonata. This is the first example in Beethoven's sonatas of the composer's placing the greatest emphasis on the finale.

Tovey's analysis of this 285-bar section reveals that it's a rondo with a development section in place of a second episode;[6] there's also a great deal of contrapuntal activity without Beethoven's ever getting anything too serious in the way of canon or fugue going. But the textures here are dense, and the movement is witty and eventful. Toward the end, Beethoven builds to a big climax, then brings back the theme of the Adagio, stirring the listener's emotions once more, unexpectedly, with that great melody, then races to a spirited ending.

The famous C-sharp Minor Sonata, Op. 27 No. 2, acquired its nickname in the middle of the nineteenth century from a German critic, Ludwig Rellstab, who wrote that the first movement suggested a boat, by moonlight, on Lake Lucerne. There can hardly be a more misleading example of one man's impression coloring a great work of art. It's really best when listening to this extraordinary work to try to put the moon and water out of your mind and discipline yourself to hear it as music, and music alone.

Like its companion piece in Op. 27, Beethoven conceived No. 2 as a single, unified arc. The structure of the C-sharp Minor Sonata is weighted toward its third-movement finale, the longest movement both in score and playing time, and its emotional climax as well. The first movement is gravely beautiful, the second, a brief, lyric interlude. But the import of the finale, a headlong rush in sonata form, is unmistakably tragic. The hypnotic opening section casts so great a spell that some listeners seem satisfied with that alone, or perhaps with getting comfortably stuck in its very genuine pleasures. But remember that the first two movements are wind-ups for the devastating finale.

Even if you know the first movement, it's good to try to hear it afresh, because it remains a remarkably bold and profound musical expression. Which specific affect it expresses is difficult to say, but neither joy nor struggle with the possibility of triumph seems to fit. The movement consists, as Tovey says, of a "continuous melody on an enormous scale."[7] The keyboard texture consists of three parts: first, three tolling notes, sometimes deep in the left hand, that carry the melody. Then, right-hand notes echo and amplify the melodic strand. Finally, there is the endless stream of triplets, the three-note figures that create steady movement yet also paradoxically add to the tranquility of the piece. The texture is therefore fairly light, even with the nearly continuous sound of the melody in the bass. Beethoven also instructs that the performer should play "with extreme delicacy."

The opening measures form a prelude; the actual melody begins at measure 4, with a thick chord in the left hand and the tolling figure in the right. Almost immediately, Beethoven moves boldly through distant keys, reining the melody in to slow notes. Around the middle of the movement, he anchors the left hand to one note, suspending melodic activity but building tension and letting the triplets wander harmonically. Finally the tolling melody returns; listen to the richness of the sonority as the melody rumbles calmly two octaves below the harmonizing notes in the right hand. The music moves with imperturbable grandeur to its quiet conclusion, with the tolling figure sounding six times in the bass. In this remarkable feat of musical construction, Beethoven juggles tension, calm, texture, sonority, and deepest expression with absolute mastery.

The second movement is a short essay in lilting dance rhythm, made up of paired phrases. Its mood is wistful, veering toward melancholy. The trio, set deeper on the keyboard, involves more syncopated figuration.

It's easy enough to describe the structure of the third and closing movement: it's in sonata form. And while it's best when looking at a musical work to stay with descriptions and analysis that are more or less objective, sometimes, as with this tremendous and terrible movement, Beethoven makes restraint difficult. This is music of towering passion and power, in which a mature Beethoven reveals the full force of his imaginative genius. The emotional and dramatic agendas of the music must be given their due.

Beethoven's tempo indication is *presto agitato*—quick and agitated—so everything moves fast, and the mood is stormy from beginning to end. The first subject is a hurricane of arpeggios that rush up the keyboard, ending in two sharp chords. The next figure is an anxious melody in eighth notes for the left hand that spins itself out under a trembling accompaniment in the right; then the initial figure returns. The second theme is what takes the place of a protagonist in this drama, a sharply profiled, memorable melody in the right hand over a rushing broken-chord figure in the left that soon dissolves into furious trills, crashing chords, and rushing scales. These devolve into another strong new element, a series of staccato chords for both hands that sounds like panting. The exposition ends on a series of high Ds, which Beethoven reaches by arpeggiated grace notes. In the development, the composer makes much of the sharply profiled second theme, putting it in the left hand and giving it a more baritonal or cello-like quality. The doom-laden passage over a rumbling figure deep in the bass that prepares the way back to the main theme seems to foreshadow Wagner. The recapitulation brings back all of the familiar but still terrifying material. As lead-in to the coda, Beethoven adds two massive arpeggiated chords, then a cadenza-like passage, before the final, fearful sweep up and down the keyboard and two savage concluding chords.

Our last sonata of this grouping, composed in the productive year 1801, is the D Major, Op. 28. Nicknamed the "Pastoral," this rich and polished work is longer, more regular in form, and more tranquil than its three companion pieces of Opp. 26 and 27. It's played relatively seldom but still has much to offer. Beethoven's publisher bestowed the nickname, finding references to pastoral musical traditions in the first movement and especially the rocking rhythm and bagpipe-like drone of the opening bars of the rondo.

The opening movement is in a broadly conceived sonata form. Beethoven begins with a quietly pulsing D deep in the left hand over which the calm and beautiful first subject enters as though floating. The second theme begins with temporizing chords above bumpy repeated notes, then moves to an ecstatic, swaying melodic sequence in which the tune in the right is harmonized deep in the left and carried forward rhythmically by rippling figuration in the middle of the keyboard. There's an angry minor passage in the development, but the phrases soon turn quizzical as the composer slows the tempo considerably in preparation for the reprise of the opening material.

The slow movement is in ordinary aria form, but it is utterly original in expression. The composer spins out his melancholy tune over a march rhythm, giving the movement the quality of a processional; there are also some pungent dissonances. Equally memorable is the middle section, based on a bouncing rhythm that can readily get stuck in one's head. And in the coda, Beethoven follows the unusual procedure of combining material from both sections, then dissolving it all in a striking concluding phrase. The effect of this spectral movement on Schumann seems clear and powerful. The scherzo, too, seems proto-Schumannesque, especially in the anxious second phrase, which anticipates a passage from the younger composer's *Aufschwung* ("Soaring"), one of the *Fantasiestücke*, Op. 12. The trio is based on a racing tune in B minor. The movement is another wonderful example of Beethoven's ability to create music of substance from almost nothing: listen to and consider how spare the main theme is, and how satisfying the structure the composer builds around it.

The pastoral element finally enters in a significant way in the big closing rondo. First, the 6/8 time signature is one traditionally associated with rustic music; countless examples of it can be found in Bach, and the custom was old when he made use of it. It's a lilting rhythm that Beethoven gives to the left hand in a droning figure, above which the perky main theme enters in the right. But you will notice that the rhythm is powerful and difficult to resist. Graceful arpeggios lead to the first episode, another example of the many faces of 6/8 time. A second episode starts in a hopping rhythm but moves to a big climax. The long and impressive coda opens with a phrase in a melting sonority, then Beethoven speeds up to end this fine but underappreciated sonata on a brilliant note.

The High Middle Period

Sonatas 16–23

W ith the exception of the two short works composed in the mid-1790s and published in 1805 as Op. 49, the eight sonatas we'll examine in this chapter come from 1802 to 1806, the high phase of Beethoven's middle period. Included among the group are two of the most famous and popular of the series—indeed, of his entire oeuvre—No. 21, the "Waldstein," Op. 53, and No. 23, the "Appassionata," both huge in scale and force. But in between these two falls one of the most unusual and least-known, the Op. 54; three brilliant and varied sonatas of Op. 31 round out the group.

This was one of the most difficult periods in Beethoven's life, when his deafness was deepening and tightening its grip. Anxiety about other ailments, some real, others imagined, often overtook him, too. His relationships with other people, always troubled, became touchier as gloom and paranoia grew. He considered suicide but rejected it in the Heiligenstadt Testament, written in 1802 (see chapter 2). Some of the music of these years shows the massive strain under which he worked, with works for piano and other ensembles—the "Kreutzer" Sonata, Op. 47, for piano and violin; the Piano Concerto No. 3; and above all the Symphony No. 3—showing signs of almost constant struggle. In this era subtlety sometimes cedes place to power, though the Op. 31 and Op. 54 sonatas have much to say in an understated way.

Since the little Op. 49 sonatas predate the rest and are written in an earlier style, it makes sense to listen to them first. They were apparently ten years old and sitting unpublished in Beethoven's portfolio when in 1805 his brother Carl Caspar got his hands on them and published them for his own profit. Both have two movements and are considered sonatinas rather than full-fledged sonatas, and yet they are fine works, worthy of serious consideration and enjoyment.

The G Minor Sonata opens with a plangent and memorable melody in a moderate tempo over a close left-hand accompaniment in thirds. The consoling second theme, in B-flat major, emerges in more flowing styles in both hands. In the development, Beethoven subjects the second theme to some minor-key treatment. The movement ends with a coda, only seven bars long but of great beauty, which turns to G major, the key of the concluding rondo, at the very end. That rondo, in an unusual form, is mostly light in texture but is in no sense a miniature. The main idea is a rollicking G major theme in the 6/8 time and "hunting" mood of Mozart, but Beethoven changes keyboard figuration and tone color rapidly with racing episodes in G minor. As in the first movement, the coda is short, but its open-air feeling gives an interesting and effective end to this lovely short work.

The material of the G Major Sonata (or Sonatina), Op. 49 No. 2, seems perhaps just a bit less personal than that of its companion. The opening group consists of two brisk, bustling ideas, while the second theme opens more thoughtfully, then ends with a fine sequence of falling triplets that echoes the closing phrase of the first theme. The brief development section of thirteen bars takes the opening theme into minor regions. Using a charming melody he would later deploy in his singular Septet for Clarinet, Horn, Bassoon, Violin, Viola, Cello and Double Bass, Op. 20, of 1799, the closing rondo in "Tempo di Menuetto" with two energetic episodes, is one of the master's most easygoing movements. Beethoven ends the work with a dainty coda.

Beethoven composed the three important sonatas that make up Op. 31 in 1802. They are the last sonatas to be published in a group, but they burst at the seams with individuality. Each work has its own distinctive character, as Rosen observes, "particularly by their opening movements by which they are largely identified: comic, tragic, and lyric."[1] All three also share a peculiar nervous, high-strung quality, perhaps reflecting the tension that affected the composer as he worked. And while the first and third of the set look back in certain stylistic ways, these are fully middle-period Beethoven.

Perhaps the backward-looking quality of the G Major Sonata, Op. 31 No. 1, puts off modern audiences, because the work is among the least popular of all the thirty-two piano sonatas. The opening movement's comedy, referred to by Rosen, may be obvious only to music professionals, although its humorous tone should be clear enough to any attentive listener. Beethoven's main comic effect is the rhythmic hiccup or stutter that sets off the opening theme, a sequence of slightly pompous chords that never synchronize. The composer follows this with a long section of ceremonious, slightly fussy passagework that continues the mock pomposity of the opening phrase. The second theme is a racy tune in the unusual key of B major, which quickly oscillates to B minor, then zigzags back to B major again as it passes from hand to hand. Beethoven's choice of keys is important here because it represents a departure from classical sonata procedure, but one the composer would employ to great effect, for example in the "Waldstein" Sonata, Op. 53, as we'll soon see and hear. (For those interested in these matters, D major would be the normal key for a second theme of a composition in G major; Beethoven's move to B major/minor, a third up from G, is an early example of his interest in key relationships based on the interval of the third, and one he would continue to exploit over the course of his career.) The other joke in this masterful movement is the hanging phrases that conclude it. Note, as you listen, to the questioning phrases Beethoven extracts from three chords lifted from the opening theme, which he brings back for a final coy incarnation in the coda. They're met by a single thunderous reply, followed by two soft chords that seem the musical equivalent of a double-take.

The slow movement, another operatic take-off in the manner of Op. 22 and Op. 27 No. 1, is surely the part of the sonata that's hardest for most modern listeners to grasp. Its florid ornamentation seems way over the top, and there's also an element of parody, at a rarefied level, of the Italian operatic style that was on the verge of becoming *bel canto*. With a playing time of nearly ten minutes, it's a bit long for an inside joke. The form of the movement is that of a simple ABA aria, and the melody is a fairly standard tune in the Italian-opera style. What's unusual is the lavish, nervous, trill-laden ornamentation under which Beethoven buries the tune from the beginning and the jittery accompaniment over which it's laid. The middle section is more graceful, almost like a ballet, and on its return the main melody is subjected to even wilder decoration. It's strange music to most ears, and perhaps always has been, except to those with a grasp of Italian operatic history and style. But one can begin to appreciate it with time and a little experience listening to the operas of Rossini, Bellini, and Donizetti.

Neglect of Op. 31 No. 1 deprives audiences of the opportunity to hear one of Beethoven's most beautiful and sophisticated rondos. Based on an elegant, rolling melody, Beethoven combines rondo and sonata form in a suave hybrid that was a major inspiration for Schubert, who leaned heavily but successfully on it for the last movement of his own great Piano Sonata in A Major, D. 959. Beethoven speeds up in a whirling coda, where, as in the first movement, he condenses his material to next to nothing in a comical ending: suddenly the music just disappears.

The Sonata No. 17 in D Minor, Op. 31 No. 2, the only one of the thirty-two in that key, is nicknamed the "Tempest," from a story, now considered apocryphal, that Beethoven replied, "Read Shakespeare's *Tempest*," when asked by one of the boldest fools in history what the sonata was "about." As abstract music, it's obviously not about anything, in a verbal sense; the tale of the nickname has become a good lesson in the perils of extramusical associations. But within the legend lies a germ of truth, a response to the undeniable sense of dramatic narrative in this towering work that stands as perhaps the greatest in the series of sonatas composed by Beethoven up to this point.

Beethoven radically alters sonata form to suit his needs in the dramatic first movement. Convulsive changes of tempo and affect that range from dreamy to furious characterize the entire structure, with the dominant mood mixing anxiety and despair. Nor does the composer provide release from its musical and emotional mazes. The opening gesture is a slow, mysterious arpeggio on an A major chord, from which what seems to be the main theme emerges, an anxious and agitated figure in D minor that ends with a slow, expressive turn; we soon discover that the entire indivisible cluster is the first theme. Immediately the same sequence follows in another key, leading into a long, transitional passage in which a stern figure in a crisp rhythm leaps from the bass. It alternates with a pleading, legato one in the right hand, the two bound together by quivering triplets played alternately by the right and left hands. Beethoven packs this material into two pages, which take just over a minute's playing time. The fretful second subject, in A minor, continues the anxious mood, then plunges into the heart of the keyboard for a series of powerful chords. Beethoven ends the exposition with a potent sequence of somber unisons deep in the bass; the material is then repeated.

The remarkable development section is launched by three slow arpeggios, like those that open the work, but taking the key far away from D minor, as though the composer were improvising; it then suddenly explodes into the transitional material of the opening. This evolves into a sequence of thick, twisting tremolos, which finally quiet down to a passage of somber chords and unison notes. The opening chord of the sonata reappears, leading us to think we've reached firm formal ground with a normal recapitulation. But instead, there's a long, slow, sorrow-laden recitative, played softly by the right hand with the pedal echoing, as though from an infinite distance. The agitated D minor part of the main theme returns, trailed as usual by a broken chord, but this leads to another sorrowful recitative. Their dramatic effect is potent; the music practically speaks. We're impelled to wonder: what *is* it about?

Four hollow, detached chords and wild passagework, played *pianissimo*, then repeated louder, and finally heard a third time *fortissimo* make us expect that an explosion, a release, is finally at hand; but what follows is only the fretful second theme. Beethoven then deploys the closing sequence to lead into a brief but majestic coda in which the composer emphasizes the D minor tonality in quiet chords in the right hand over a rumbling figure in the left. The movement ends on two solemn tonic chords.

The glorious Adagio, an oasis in B-flat major, opens, like the first movement, with an arpeggio. The first subject of this songful sonata-form essay is a noble, hymnlike melody, which Beethoven embellishes with quasi-orchestral flourishes, including mock drumbeats played by the left hand and echoed in the right, which in an orchestrated version would probably be played by the violins. The second theme, in a sharper walking rhythm, seems more feminine than the hymnlike opening theme but is equally noble and tranquil. The opening theme returns, embellished by sixteenth-note flourishes that pass from hand to hand and that might be called Chopinesque if they didn't predate Chopin. The composer introduces a broad new melody in the coda, as though commenting on what went before.

The time signature for the spasmodic first movement is what's called "cut time," a quick beat; the Adagio is in stately 3/4 time. To end this tragic sonata effectively, Beethoven concludes the work with a "pathetic" perpetual-motion essay in a waltzlike 3/8 time that's delicate but relentless, its steady rhythmic drive pulling the whole work together to its inevitable end. The material of the movement is economy itself: a tight four-note phrase over an arpeggiated accompaniment, with the little phrases interwoven. Beethoven's harmony is rich, though, and the tiny patterns soon link together into broad, sweeping waves. There's only one point, at the end of the long opening sequence, where the pattern reaches up for one perfectly poised sigh, actually a falling chromatic scale, before running down again. The second theme (the movement is in sonata form) is a fretful, syncopated motto in A minor that breaks the mood not at all: the irresistible rhythm hardly allows us to realize it's another tune. The development is delicate, never thunderous, but the mood remains dark throughout. The end of the sonata is desolate yet strangely graceful as a final sigh, then the four-note theme and its supporting arpeggios drop quietly off the bottom of the keyboard.

Beethoven takes the wide-ranging characteristics of the Op. 31 sonatas as a group to its furthest point in the third and last, in E-flat major. Op. 31 No. 3 differs from its companions with its brilliant personality, and all of its four movements differ from each other, as well. And, curiously, the composer found no place in this idiosyncratic four-movement work for one part that is slow. The opening movement is lyrical, founded on the yearning harmony of the opening chord; the second is a high-strung scherzo. The tranquil third movement is the last normal minuet in the piano sonatas, and the finale is a wild tarantella with which Beethoven pulls the whole thing together. There's little else like it in his output unless we jump speculatively ahead to 1825 and the B-flat Major String Quartet, Op. 130, in which the composer harnesses six movements of different characters into a whole that surprises with its ultimate coherence.

The sound of a sweetly dissonant chord that leaves the ear uncertain as to where its harmony will settle, making us wonder how it will resolve, opens the work. Music writers have come up with a few words to characterize it: conversational, questioning, or yearning all give a pretty fair sense. It is in any case soulful and unrhetorical. But that does not mean it lacks tension, and one of Beethoven's plays throughout the movement is to take the opening sequence and throw it into different harmonic lights and shadows. Ultimately he resolves the opening chordal sequence on a melodic phrase that ends conventionally in E-flat major. The rhythm of the opening figure is then set over a pulsing accompaniment and a trill-laden sequence; Beethoven rounds out the opening group with a busy theme in eighth notes. The second theme is a rather nervous Haydnesque melody over an Alberti (broken-chord) left hand, which dissolves into fluttery passagework for the right hand, then recovers its poise and resumes. Clouds pass in the development as Beethoven takes the opening theme, which has an inherent heaviness owing to its thick, chordal nature, through some dark keys. It's also a fine example of a working-out where the composer breaks themes apart into sections of melodies to pit against one another. The mood of the movement is far from tragic, and often seems to look back affectionately to eighteenth-century ways.

While the opening movement is predominantly lyrical, it has a rich strain of nervousness that Beethoven brings to the fore in the second-movement scherzo. This, the strangest movement in the work, is not a typical scherzo for two important formal reasons: it's in sonata form rather than the usual scherzo-trio-scherzo structure, and its time signature is 2/4, not the normal triple meter. So Beethoven uses the title to describe its playful nature rather than its form, as he did with the finale of Op. 14 No. 2. His tightly wound nervous system is on full display in this busy, technically difficult movement, where a light touch is called for as one hand or the other, and often both, are called on to play staccato. The first theme has a steady rise, then a fall, but it's set over jumpy patterns in the left hand; the even friskier second theme consists of tiny gestures in the left hand decorated by figuration set high in the right. Note how even the explosive chords Beethoven uses to jump to new keys are loud but very short. The development contains some comical swoops, and the coda consists of bare octaves falling to an acrobatic closing cadence.

The scherzo occupies the place of a slow movement in this unusual work, so Beethoven uses the menuetto to fill its place as a moment of lyrical reflection. This beautiful movement consists of an expansive melody, richly harmonized, in the outer sections, balanced by a trio with a more playful but still tranquil theme built on chords. The composer compresses the rhythm in the central section of the trio, confusing us by making it sound for a moment as if he were in a two-beat pulse. And he gives the movement an unexpected ending with a coda in a hesitant rhythm and darkened harmonic coloring.

The tensions accumulated in the first and second movements are still unresolved; even the apparently calm menuetto ended ambiguously. Beethoven clears the decks with a brilliant virtuoso showpiece. The finale is a wild sonata-form movement in a tarantella rhythm; Schubert, once again, borrowed the idea for the finale to his C Minor Piano Sonata, D. 958. Everything happens quickly: the tempo, *presto con fuoco*, means "quickly, with fire." It opens with a sliding theme in the right hand over the furious scurrying of triplets in the left, followed instantly by a new idea in a prancing rhythm. The second group is based on syncopated, aggressively repeated notes high in the right hand. The movement consists of alternations of the thematic elements, sometimes stated genially, other times in mock fury, but always with unrelenting forward motion. Near the end, the music comes to rest on two grandly arpeggiated chords before racing to its end.

Before reading about the next sonata, the "Waldstein," take a moment to listen to track 3 on the accompanying CD, the brief Bagatelle in A-flat Major, Op. 33 No. 7, of 1802. A full discussion of the bagatelle can be found in chapter 11, but as you'll hear, the similarities between the themes of the bagatelle and the first movement of the sonata are considerable. The bagatelle, one of Beethoven's wildest creations, seethes with the same energy as that animating the sonata's first movement. And although the bagatelle has a clear and firm structure, it sounds close at times to spinning of control, while the composer holds a tighter rein on his material over the course of the sonata's long first movement.

The Sonata No. 21 in C Major, Op. 53, composed in 1803 and 1804—the "Waldstein"—is one of the most famous of the series. It's nicknamed for its dedicatee, Count Ferdinand von Waldstein, one of Beethoven's oldest friends and patrons, whose relationship with the composer went back to the years in Bonn. The sonata, which occupies tracks 4 and 5 on the CD that accompanies this book, is remarkable for many reasons, among them the vast new scale on which Beethoven works and its ferocious power. The "Waldstein" is also a work in which melody takes a back seat to rhythm and harmony: this is not a work of long-spun tunes, but rather of nearly generic, blocklike material, which Beethoven propels with driving rhythms and shifting, often startling harmonies. Even the dynamics—the volume of the music, the play of loud against soft—seem as important as the thematic material itself. Of course Beethoven could come up with long, moving melodies at will, but those were not what he needed for the highly dynamic, sometimes rough treatment he accords them here. The "Waldstein" is also a virtuoso showpiece, of obvious difficulty to play, and ought to be overwhelmingly effective in performance.

The "Waldstein" is basically set in two huge movements, a sonata-form opening section and a Rondo. The opening movement, vast in scale and displaying a more driving energy than any of its predecessors, has all the middle-period power a Beethoven fan could hope for; the gigantic, glittering Rondo also breaks new ground in its size, force, and scope. In place of a slow movement, Beethoven prefaces the Rondo with a twenty-eight-bar Introduzione at a very slow tempo. His original plan for the sonata included a lyrical, highly ornamented slow movement later published separately as the *Andante favori*, WoO 57 (see chapter 11).[2] But Beethoven decided that its easygoing ways did not fit into his streamlined, harmonically forward-looking conception for this sonata, so he dropped the Andante and made the inspired addition of the profound Introduzione.[3]

The distant thunder of the first movement's exposition sounds like no sonata opening Beethoven had ever written. Certainly the wild, *pianissimo* throbbing of the opening two measures, followed by a falling melodic fragment (CD Track 4, 0:04) in the middle of the keyboard, then a sudden reply from high up (0:05), seems more elemental than musical, even primitive, like the racing of one's own pulse. (Three other middle-period main themes with the same pulsing energy are those of the first movements of the String Quartet No. 7 in F Major, Op. 59 No. 1, of 1806 and the contemporaneous Symphony No. 3—and, of course, the Bagatelle in A-flat Major, Op. 33 No. 7). The melodic figure is repeated, in rising volume over quickly changing harmony. By 0:12–0:13 the volume has risen considerably; note as well the E-flat at 0:17, because it hints at C minor and at the harmonic instability that, along with the brutal rhythm, drives this powerful movement forward. At 0:21 Beethoven restates the opening theme as sixteenth notes, giving it a new, slightly easier, rippling sound. This merges at 0:34 into a long transitional passage in a new harmony (veering excitingly between E minor and E major) that sets the stage for the second subject.

This chordal sequence enters at 0:52, falling and then rising in a type of melodic pattern Beethoven employed regularly. It seems melodious after the thunderous opening material but is fairly neutral if you compare it to the articulate second subject of any first movement in Op. 31. Like that of Op. 31 No. 1, however, it's a major third up from its tonic, or home key, here C major, so it's in the distantly related (and therefore unusual) key of E major. The effect of Beethoven's daring move is to expand the scale of the movement beyond the normal classical harmonic pattern, which would move predictably to G major, then back to C major. And this new freedom Beethoven took had a major impact on composers who followed. Triplets enter in the right hand to decorate the second theme (1:05), then dominate the texture in a transitional passage in which Beethoven builds excitement again by means of shorter note values, intensified rhythms, and increased volume. At 1:37 we reach the beginning of a long cadence, or passage where harmonic and rhythmic tensions are supposed to settle. But instead Beethoven presents us with a wild phrase of sixteenth notes storming upward over a furious rhythm pounded out in thick chords in the left hand, finally thinning the texture and calming things down just a bit over these closing bars of the exposition. Note especially the new melodic figure that enters at 1:59 and dominates the proceedings until the end.

The entire exposition is now repeated, beginning at 2:15 and running through 4:30.

Beethoven opens the exceptionally long development section with a continuation of the melodic phrase that closed the exposition, but he soon moves to tossing condensed melodic fragments from the opening together above the opening rhythmic figure (4:40 to 5:00). He loosens these up in preparation for a long, fantasia-like passage at the heart of the development (5:10 to about 5:48), where he drives the triplets that accompanied the second theme grandly through several keys. Then, just as Beethoven appears to be settling things down, he undermines the calm, building harmonic and rhythmic tension from 5:48 to 5:54. In perhaps the maddest passage in the sonata—so far ahead of its time that Prokofiev might have written it—Beethoven runs rising fragments reminiscent of the right hand's opening activity over a motoric repeated figure in the left—shades of our Bagatelle, Op. 33 No. 7.

A massive scale in contrary motion (where the hands move in opposite directions) at 6:15 leads to the recapitulation, which enlarges somewhat the material set forth in the exposition. For example, the falling phrase at 6:32 is echoed by one in another key, then there's yet another scampering incarnation starting at 6:42. Note also that the second theme comes back in A major (7:19) and, in another expansion, is immediately echoed in A minor at 7:26. In keeping with the outsized dimensions of the work, Beethoven adds a huge coda beginning at 8:45 with the opening material, now in the very remote key of D-flat major. Here the music takes on a more open, concerto-like texture, with octaves (9:02 and 9:08) interspersed with broad scales (starting at 9:04) and finally winding up in a passage resembling a cadenza (9:25 to 9:38). If you compare this passage to the cadenza Beethoven interpolated into the first movement of Op. 2 No. 3, you will quickly realize how much more artfully this one is proportioned and integrated into the musical texture. The second theme returns for the last time, then the opening pulsation at 10:11, followed by another powerful scale in contrary motion. Four sharp chords end the movement in high excitement.

Although just over a page in the score, the Introduzione that prefaces the concluding Rondo moves at such a slow tempo that its playing time is nearly four minutes; it's densely woven and deep, too. The form is a free, lyrical contrivance of Beethoven's, used here and here only, though it did bear fruit in later "shadow" slow movements that lead into finales, as in the Piano Sonata No. 28 in A Major, Op. 101, and the String Quartet in C-sharp Minor, Op. 131. Cast in three broad sections, the movement begins deep on the keyboard, with a gesture that reaches upward and then ends in three tranquil chords; this is repeated in another key (CD Track 5, 0:20), then once again in a different key (0:39). The tempo is so slow that the music seems barely to move (and the pianist Jenö Jandó takes it faster than many); the effect is deeply mysterious. At 1:25 the second portion of the movement begins, a more fluid and expressive element in the style of an arioso, or melodious phrase, also reaching upward. Note the beautiful rising tail it trails on both appearances (1:36 and 1:51). The music achieves real eloquence in the three measures, from 1:57 to 2:20, where the opening figure returns, now marked by a turn deep in the bass (2:28). The upward-reaching figure of the opening recurs in the right hand along with the turn in the left from 2:57 to 3:17. The music seems frozen in place, but then the left begins to move faster, the pattern in the right breaks apart, and at 3:27 Beethoven gently moves the harmony toward G major, the dominant of C major, the key of the Rondo. The role of the dominant key is to create anticipation, and that's what gives the final cadence (3:47 to 3:50) its expectant tone and clarifies the role of this movement as a preface—an Introduzione—to the Rondo, which follows without pause.

The soaring main theme enters high on the keyboard over a rippling accompaniment. As in the first movement, it is a tune that's memorable, even hypnotic, but simple, answering the composer's need for something that will stand up well to aggressive treatment. And although almost blinding in its C majorness, it also displays a tendency toward C minor, as evidenced by the E-flat at 4:08, then again at 4:37 and 4:41; over and over throughout this long movement you will hear the melody oscillate between purest C major and then that tug toward C minor that makes everything else seem all the brighter. A long trill enters at 4:43; such trills also form an important part of this movement's glittering sound. The first episode, a burly, toccata-like passage dominated by triplets, begins at 4:55; it's also notable for hammered octaves. This busily spins itself out, and at 5:33 Beethoven states the main theme three times in octaves, emphasizing the leisurely long-short-short rhythm of its first three notes. This being a rondo, the main theme returns in unaltered form at 5:51.

The second episode, a mock-furious affair in C minor typical of the rondo form, begins at 6:51, characterized by hammered octaves and rushing triplets that pass from hand to hand. Beethoven ends this on five bare hammered Cs, then, at 7:38, states the main theme in full harmony. The long passage that follows, ending only at 9:12, is a long development-like sequence—even though this is a rondo—in which vast harmonic distances are traversed. Beethoven does his traveling in various ways: note the hypnotic passage beginning at 7:57 in which syncopated chords shift gently over the bass line, reminiscent of a similar phrase in the last movement of Op. 10 No. 3. But his chief strategy here is to run rainbow-like scales and arpeggios (starting at 8:10) over the short-short-long rhythm in the left. At last the main theme returns (9:12) for its final appearance, merging at 9:43 into the beginning of the huge and stunning coda.

Beethoven kicks the coda off with the triplets of the second episode, soon giving them to both hands in a long, glorious passage that ends at 10:19, in a series of chords with the feeling of a dying fall; then, at 10:48, he breaks into *prestissimo*, the fastest of all tempos, with the main theme shimmering high on the keyboard. Everything moves very quickly now. A new rhythmic pattern in the left hand at 11:00 adds more excitement, as if it were needed. The short-short-long pattern supports some majestic triplets starting at 11:18, and at 11:40 a passage legendary for its difficulty begins. These are scales played in octaves *glissando*, by the player sliding his or her fingers across the keys. This was possible only with the lighter action of the fortepiano of 1804; it can't be done on a modern piano, where it has to be taken note by note, but it's still pretty effective when well executed. At 11:50 another long trill begins as Beethoven plays the theme out over exquisite, rapidly shifting harmonies. At 12:25 the theme and short-short-long rhythm appear triumphantly together, and the work races to its end in thundering C major chords.

Sandwiched between the immensities of the "Waldstein" and the "Appassionata," the little Sonata in F Major, Op. 54, of 1804 is mostly loved by those who know it and otherwise ignored. Since everything about this subtle two-movement work of delicate humor and profound musicianship is unusual, Op. 54 simply needs to be taken on its own terms. It resembles and points toward the achievements of its two-part siblings, Opp. 78 and 90, distinguished sonatas of 1809 and 1814 respectively that no longer fit the middle-period style but follow their own paths. Some of the compression and abrupt shifts in the first movement even anticipate the master's late style.

Beethoven's tempo marking for the first movement is *In tempo d'un Menuetto*—in the tempo of a minuet. This is not precisely the same as saying that it is a minuet, and that opens an ironic distance between creator and creation. It's music *about* the minuet, much as Ravel would compose dance pieces *about* old forms, including the minuet, in his piano suite *Le tombeau de Couperin*. But the opening theme and first musical paragraph—the first thematic group—are of course highly minuet-like, the latter embellished in its final phrase with turns and trills. The bumptious trio that erupts in staccato triplets is clearly comical, finally playing itself out in a curious repeated phrase known as an *ostinato* that jumps from high in the right hand to deep in the left before reintroducing the minuet theme, now embroidered with comically fussy turns and repeated grace notes. Out of nowhere the trio reappears, ending on a beautiful triplet flourish; then the minuet comes back again, heavily decorated. Its appearance ends in a striking phrase marked by delicately leaping trills and expressive, quasi-spoken notes. The coda, unexpectedly fervent after the comedy that went before, begins with the opening phrase being presented over pulsing triplets in the bass, then intensifying in harmony and ornamentation, and finally swelling up to a massive, exotically lush dominant chord in throbbing triplets before falling back in a demure F major cadence.

The second movement of Op. 54 is difficult to describe because Beethoven makes up his own form, a musical and intellectual puzzle. And to dwell on its complexity does no justice to its constant, rippling beauty. The movement is basically a toccata-like perpetual-motion study in two voices murmuring delicately together in counterpoint.

Sometimes you will hear them moving in the same direction, at others not. The finale of Op. 26 will give you some sense of what it's like, but this is far more daring in its structure and harmony. That unusual structure includes a long development section, which Beethoven repeats in a rare procedure; at its center you'll hear a rocking figure in the left hand. From a harmonic standpoint, he roams subtly but with absolute freedom. Until the exciting coda the tempo is moderate and the volume mostly restrained. And the coda, in a faster tempo, is fiery. But the best strategy for a first-timer is probably just to listen to this complex movement and soak up its quiet daring and neo-Bachian beauty.

An unscientific analysis suggests that the Sonata No. 23 in F Minor, Op. 57—the "Appassionata"—is now the most performed of the thirty-two, at least on compact disc. The popularity of this potent work, completed in 1806, may be well deserved but is surprising, too, because the sonata is one of Beethoven's darkest creations, not merely passionate, but tragic from start to finish. (The nickname was given by the first publisher, irritating the composer.) Certainly its material possesses a unity that makes the sonata a compelling whole, alongside a turbulent and cathartic power that must speak to the same part of us that responds to *King Lear*, because Beethoven's music is just as comfortless. Like its sun-drenched sibling the "Waldstein," Op. 57 is also very difficult to play, and exciting and effective when well performed. The "Appassionata" is built in three sections: a large opening movement in sonata form in quick tempo and of the most turbulent character, followed by a central slow movement in the form of a theme with four variations, at a moderate speed. Though in a major key, this is nevertheless quite contained in expression, offering little relief from the prevailing dark tone. It is connected with another stormy sonata-form essay, this one in perpetual motion; Beethoven ends the work with a huge and tumultuous coda.

The opening theme, in a fluid 12/8 meter, softly outlines the F minor chord by hands two octaves apart in a hollow, mysterious sonority, rising to a trill; Beethoven repeats the sinuous theme, which can hardly be called a melody, in G-flat major, followed by the trills and a new four-note motto, much like the famous one from the first movement of the Symphony No. 5, in a brief, tense dialogue. The opening phrase is then completed by fierce, thundering chords, and a transitional section of leaping figures over pulsing triplets in the left hand sets the stage for the second subject. Although this theme is in A-flat major, Beethoven constructs it in nearly the same rhythm as the first theme and so similar in feeling that it does not present the usual contrast, but rather a sense of continuity, offering a fine example of the aesthetic unity that makes this sonata so remarkable. Like the first theme, the second has a sequence of trills followed by falling triplets before an idea with a genuinely new profile enters. This is a furious tune buried in sixteenth notes, with a hammered, rising figure in the left hand that rises before melting into a grief-laden closing sequence.

Beethoven opens the development by taking the questioning sequence from the first page of the sonata and places it in different keys, casting it into different lights. What it gets for an answer is the opening theme, now banged out loudly to a trembling accompaniment, then pitched terrifyingly around falling arpeggios. The second theme appears, soon opening into colossal, anguished arpeggios, followed by the four-note motto and breathless triplets. In the recapitulation Beethoven piles on more vast arpeggios in which the limits of expression seems to be reached, then stretched. The four-note motto leads into a quickening of tempo in which the second theme returns, again in minor key; then comes a sequence of hammered chords of the utmost ferocity. Suddenly the volume drops, and the main theme undulates around a trembling sixteenth-note figure before dropping away at the very bottom of the keyboard, ending the movement as it began, in mystery and terror.

Beethoven sets the tempo for the second movement at *andante con moto*, an easy walking pace that is not really slow, and therefore not the pause for breath a true Adagio might provide. Instead, it's a theme in D-flat major with four variations, with an inconclusive close that leads directly into the finale. The theme is a contained, almost stiff melody, expressed as chords and in two parts, that seems to keep falling back into itself—nothing like the opulent tunes that open the first movement of Op. 26 or the Op. 34 variations. Again, Beethoven's intention is not to allow much in the way of lyrical relief. The first variation continues the restrained mood in setting the melody uneasily against a syncopated bass. In the second, Beethoven loosens up a bit, offering a chamber music–like texture as the left hand sings the tune, cello-like, under a steady flow of sixteenth notes in the right hand. The third variation is the brightest in tone of all as the right hand plays the melody legato over an excited accompaniment in the left; the hands then switch the material, with the right taking the fast accompaniment. Then Beethoven cools matters down, anticipating the drama and violence of the approaching third movement in the fourth variation, which presents the theme glumly, in a manner close to the original.

But instead of closing with the expected D-flat major chord, Beethoven introduces a different one, played once slowly and dreamily, then snapped violently in an arpeggio. A new chord banged out vehemently twelve times follows at once and marks the opening of the finale. Some introductory sixteenth notes trickle out high up, followed by a flood, and a few bars later the perpetual-motion underlay of the first subject of this tremendous sonata-form movement is under way. It consists of running passagework alternating with a two-note motto in a stinging rhythm, followed by a more extended version of the motto in moaning thirds. Beethoven closes the group out with a shuddering figure in sixteenth notes. The second subject, a circular pattern also in thirds, follows without pause, offering another example of the sonata's thematic and dramatic unity. The material is rounded out by a furious sequence of six thick, dissonant chords that play a major role as the movement progresses.

Beethoven puts his gripping material through some fascinating permutations in the development section, where the second theme dominates, before reaching a frantic peak. The long passage where Beethoven prepares for the recapitulation culminates in a titanic near-collapse and halt before he starts up again. And here Beethoven does the oddest thing: just as this headlong music has reestablished momentum, the composer indicates a repeat of the development and the opening of the recapitulation. In other words, the player goes back and takes another turn around the block instead of heading off the cliff, which, thanks to the impetus of the movement, seemed imminent. He followed the same procedure in the second movement of Op. 54, where the peculiar maneuver worked well; here it seems a mistake of heroic proportions. For many pianists, Beethoven's scores are sacred, with all repeats taken, and many fine recorded performances include this repeat. Two that don't are by Solomon and Maria João Pires.

As usual, the recapitulation includes certain expansions of material, but basically the themes are now headed swiftly toward the final catastrophe: the six closing chords catch into a whirlwind of accelerating passagework, and suddenly Beethoven introduces a furious new idea, led by savage chords, then fierce staccato chords in a stamping dance. The effect is as though he is attempting to block the inevitable by throwing something new and different in its way, but the unstoppable tidal arpeggios immediately return. On the final page the terrible forces the composer has summoned seem almost to pass beyond his control, fulfilling the cataclysm inevitable from the sonata's first note.

Five Transitional Sonatas

Beethoven wrote the five sonatas covered in this chapter over the eight years from 1809 to 1816. The first three, Opp. 78, 79, and 81a, however, date from 1809, placing them, at least in terms of chronology, firmly in the middle period. The next, Op. 90, comes from the "dry spell" year of 1814, as does the last of the group, Op. 101, of 1816. That the composer's productivity dropped is obvious: compare the eight big sonatas, Opp. 22–31, that he turned out between 1800 and 1802 with the five works here, three of which are short though certainly not light. But if you've already been struck by and enjoyed Beethoven's stylistic unpredictability, then you won't be disappointed by these five, which are as varied, and often as quirky, as they can be. Even the three sonatas from 1809 are completely different from each other in style, technique, and mood. The only consistency that may be discerned is that the grouping includes two of the always-fascinating full-scale sonatas in two movements, Opp. 78 and 90.

It is with one of these, the beautiful Sonata No. 24 in F-sharp Major, Op. 78, that Beethoven continued the series, although there's some speculation that he composed the Op. 79 sonata first.[1] Either way, Op. 78 is unusual from every point of view, from its concise, two-movement structure to its key signature: six sharps, which was extremely unusual in Beethoven's time. Indeed, this sonata seems to be his only composition in F-sharp major. The structures of both movements are singular, as we shall see. From a stylistic point of view, Op. 78 seems to fit uneasily into the middle-period category. Its closest kinship would seem to be with the Opp. 54 and 90 sonatas, all short, fundamentally lyrical works in two movements that brim with individual character. Op. 78 is an intimate work, conversational in tone, delicately proportioned, with none of the thunderous rhetoric of the signature middle-period sonatas, like the "Waldstein" or the "Appassionata." Its singular personality seems to preclude wide popularity. But most of those who know the work love it, and Op. 78 repays the listener's attention generously.

The main body of the first movement is in sonata form, but Beethoven opens the work with a remarkable passage that alters the movement's mood and proportions decisively. Marked *adagio cantabile*, or slowly and songfully, this brief phrase, which consists of a rising theme in rich harmony, sounds like the beginning of one of Beethoven's slow movements in his grandest manner. But it comes to rest immediately on an expectant turn and pause, after which the first theme comes in. The introduction, which Rosen characterizes as "a fragment of an independent slow movement . . . too short to exist on its own, but . . . complete,"[2] never recurs. Though only four bars long and occupying perhaps twenty seconds of playing time in the course of the seven-minute movement, the grave beauty of this introduction casts a far longer shadow than its brevity might lead one to expect.

Readers who have heard the "Archduke" Piano Trio, Op. 97, which Beethoven composed in 1811, may recognize that the first themes of the opening movement, while not identical, have a family resemblance: both are free, "open" tunes, noble in character, and both move in a similar easy stride. This one then breaks into delicate sixteenth-note runs, followed by triplets that turn into a chordal phrase in a memorable rhythm interspersed with pauses, which the composer expands notably later in the movement. The final element of the first theme consists of broken sixteenth notes in the right hand over a steady chord pattern of mounting harmonic intensity in the left. The second theme, which is far shorter than the first, opens with rocking triplets, which then break into more active sixteenth notes and a chord sequence that resembles the one in the first theme. A tranquilly rumbling sixteenth-note sequence in the bass pulls the material back to the beginning of the main theme. The exposition is repeated.

At only nineteen bars, the development section is brief. The composer runs the main theme through a rainbow of keys, then takes the three-note opening phrase of the melody and passes it from hand to hand over (and under) shifting harmony expressed in busy sixteenth notes, which finally take over. The recapitulation of the original material entails considerable expansion. Right from the start, for example, Beethoven doubles the delicate sixteenth-note runs that follow the main melody, and the big chord sequence that follows, too. Throughout, the sense of calm, rich fantasy is striking. At the end, Beethoven uses the same rumbling sixteenth-note phrase to introduce a short, unpretentious coda. But he also instructs the player to repeat the second part of the movement, that is, the development and recapitulation. "This should be played," as Tovey remarks, for "the movement is short and the stress on its formal aspects is a positive aesthetic gain."[3]

Beethoven constructs the second movement of two elements that contrast in rhythm and pianistic texture, and it's harmonically bold as well. That the composer constructs one of his hybrids of rondo and sonata form which still has experts in musical form scratching their heads is good for the first-time listener to know; it may then be safely placed into the background. This paradox-filled movement is delicate but vigorous and, though utterly quirky, great fun to listen to. It opens with a falling theme in a strong rhythm, but Beethoven states the harmony of the first chord ambiguously. The second thematic element, which enters at bar 12 (in case you have access to a score) is a fluttering pattern of two notes in the right hand set against a single note in the left; the right-hand figures move nervously, while the rather jazzy left hand slides along suavely below, outlining a melody that the two-note figure decorates, adding harmony. These sequences generally end in an explosive chord in a remote key, after which the pattering two-note figure takes off, unanchored by the bass line; the texture is always very light. A playful new figure, initiated as usual by an unexpected chord, consists of the two-note figure oscillating dizzily between major and minor harmony as the bass line, in an exotic new incarnation, hops about below. Beethoven brings the opening figure back again, playfully placing its phrases in different parts of the keyboard. The coda begins

with an obsessive repetition of the second phrase of the opening theme
in a thematic condensation, leading to three expectant (dominant)
chords, a glistening scale, and a brief but brilliant passage in the two-
note pattern to end the work cheerfully and without bluster.

The Sonata No. 25 in G Major, Op. 79, is far more slender than
Op. 78. Beethoven's goal here was to compose an easier piece, aimed
at the amateur market, since none of the other sonatas, except the Op.
49 pair, are playable by what is, after all, the largest group of pianists.
But he failed in his goal: although the second and third movements are
indeed easy, as he planned, the first is quite hard. Stylistically, Op. 79
fits only into its own niche; nor is it substantial enough, musically, to
anticipate the composer's late period—none of which helps the first-
time listener appreciate the work for its wonderful delicacy and wit.

Beethoven gives the first movement the interesting tempo marking *Presto alla tedesca*. Presto, obviously, means quick; *alla tedesca*
means "in the style of a German dance," which at the time Beethoven
composed this delicious movement was the *ländler*, the immediate
forerunner of the waltz. (Schubert composed both types of dances by
the dozen.) The movement flies at a breathless pace that's far faster than
any actual waltz. The exposition here is quite brief, with the composer
placing most of his emphasis on the development and recapitulation. The
movement opens directly with a memorable, surging theme in the right
hand that quickly dissolves into airy figuration high on the keyboard;
the second theme is a sequence in thirds played by the right hand over
a racing left. Beethoven concludes the opening group with a stuttering
two-note figure derived from the opening melody. The exposition is
repeated; since it's short and the tempo is fast, the two run-throughs
take just over a minute. The development is based on playful but tricky
repetitions of the two-note motto, in which Beethoven has the left hand
jump from high to low over a harmonically shifting accompaniment in
a steady rhythm played by the right. This very beautiful passage would
be hypnotic if Beethoven didn't interrupt regularly with humorously
surging scales. The opening melody returns emphatically at the start of
the recapitulation, but Beethoven roams further afield in his harmony
here and makes a few other expansions of the original material. The

development and recapitulation are then repeated. In the enchanting coda, the composer opens with the stuttering theme, tosses the main theme into the bass, then decorates it with grace notes of the pungent variety known as *accacciature*, before making it rise up to vanish high on the keyboard.

The slow movement is a gentle barcarolle in three parts. The first opens with a sighing G minor melody in chiming thirds over a simple, lilting accompaniment in the left hand. The middle section features a mournful melody in a single line over a broken-chord accompaniment in the left hand; the final section brings back the opening, expanding the expressive range of the tune into more piercing octaves at the end. This sweet movement, one of Beethoven's most unpretentious, is a delicate essay in the Italian vocal style. The witty closing rondo flies by in a flash. It consists of a melody with a strong resemblance to the opening theme of the Op. 109 sonata, though the moods of the two—the ecstasy of the later work, the comedy of this one—could hardly be more different. The first episode starts in a mock-vehement E minor, then moves to alternations of the opening phrase with brief but emphatic silences. The second episode presents an acrobatic new theme, and the final appearance of the main theme is in breathless broken triplets. In the closing passage Beethoven carries the theme up the keyboard in crescendo, then drops the volume for the final cadence, to breathtaking effect.

Sonata No. 26 in E-flat Major, Op. 81a, nicknamed "Les adieux," is dense, powerful, and fraught with intense emotions. Although it ends joyously, a good performance should leave you a bit exhausted and shaken up. Beethoven himself titled the sonata "The Farewells," but his verbal intentions were muddled from the start, and obviously there's a story behind the name. This final piano sonata of 1809 is what's known as program music, which means that it tells a story or paints a picture in tone, like Beethoven's Symphony No. 6—the "Pastoral." But instrumental program music fell into low esteem at some point in the last century; it was considered to be naive and to lack the seriousness of its purely abstract sibling. Nevertheless, it was a musical category in which many great composers, including Bach, Haydn, and Berlioz, worked comfortably. Beethoven flatly labels this sonata program music:

he subtitles the score, which paints a musical impression of a separation from his patron and friend Archduke Rudolph during a Napoleonic invasion of Austria, a *Sonate caracteristique*, meaning it's a character or descriptive piece. The composer named each of the three movements, the first being "Farewell," the second "The Absence," and the third, "The return"—titles that suggest their separate, related subjects and moods. Beethoven's own names were in German: "Das Lebewohl," "Abwesenheit," and "Das Wiedersehen"; his publisher translated them into French, in spite of Beethoven's clear instructions. The French names stuck, and although the composer complained bitterly, the damage was done. On the face of it, the sonata is very similar to Bach's early masterwork for keyboard, the *Capriccio on the Departure of a Beloved Brother.* But the resemblance between the young Bach's charming piece, where the tone painting is fairly literal, and this work by the mature Beethoven, in which emotions are more broadly drawn, is almost nil. It's uncertain whether Beethoven, an admirer and student of Bach's music, knew the capriccio.

The opening movement ("Lebewohl," "Les adieux," or "The Farewell"—take your pick) is in a densely woven sonata form with an intense and deeply serious sixteen-bar slow introduction. Beethoven begins the work with a falling three-note motto that sounds like a distant horn call; over each note the composer wrote a syllable of the word: *Le-be-wohl.* His intentions for the work could not be clearer, with the motto acting as a musical setting for his one-word lyric. This wistful sequence permeates the entire movement, returning with particular poignancy in the coda. The introduction, which is in the nature of a lyrical recitative, moves at a slow and steady pace yet is also notable for a profound sense of unrest, which Beethoven expresses through the ever-shifting, twisting harmonic fabric. As you'll hear, both the first and the second movements of Op. 81a are remarkable for their harmonic restlessness. Finally, the pattern of steady forward motion begins to break into smaller units broken by eloquent silences, preparing the way for the main body of the movement.

The impetuous first theme crashes in, in alternating long notes with two short ones trying to leap up; but pay attention when you listen to how the thick, mid-keyboard texture of the left hand line drags it continuously downward, expressing a raw, pained emotion. The next phrase, a restless melody in octaves above an urgent broken-chord accompaniment, ranges widely over the keyboard, leading to a notoriously treacherous chattering passage in which all the fingers seem to fly in different directions. The group closes with a hovering figure, alternating with harmonically ambiguous chords, then finally a play on the strong rhythm of the opening theme. Beethoven builds the second theme from the "Lebewohl" motto but transforms it by extending it over four bars and adding the hovering figure from the first group; the rest of the theme, a falling cadential phrase, is also based on the motto. The development section is one of Beethoven's strangest: his chief tactic is to fragment the first theme into a flickering motion kept in the left hand beneath a sequence of big chords, mysteriously harmonized; the effect is hesitant and disturbing. Finally the rhythm pulls it all together, and the leaps of the opening theme are restored for the recapitulation. The coda is of exceptional dimension and weight. Beethoven runs through all the main material: the "Lebewohl" motto, then a condensed version of the first theme, and finally a minor-key incarnation of the restless, wide-ranging second tune; he then takes the "Lebewohl" motto, crushing it against itself in different harmonizations, and finally underlines it with pressing eighth notes, adding a fervent character. The effect is of farewells receding audibly into the distance, and some hear, in the little staccato figures in the left hand, the clip-clop of horses' hooves.

The second movement, "Absence," reflects the sadness of separation. The opening section, which recalls the slow introduction to the first movement in its keyboard layout and harmonic restlessness, is based on a three-note motif that dominates the movement. Its tone is sad, though not tragic; the tempo, moderate, rather than really slow. A passage in quicker notes for the right hand rises, then falls. A new, more consoling idea follows, elaborately decorated, over a broken-chord accompaniment that moves into a curious staccato; this is succeeded by the main motto, reharmonized and with heavier chords added, darkening the mood. The right-hand phrase for single notes returns, leading to the main theme, now stated in plangent octaves, then in a final, quieter incarnation as it rises over a brightening harmony. The third movement—"The Return"—connects directly with the closing phrase.

To represent his immense joy, Beethoven writes in a lilting 6/8 meter and gives his movement what must be the only outing for the tempo marking *Vivacissimamente: vivace*, lively, taken to its ultimate level. This remarkable sonata-form finale is packed with thematic material, but the tempo is so fast and the mood so wild that you may be overwhelmed by it all the first few times you hear the sonata. First a long phrase of busy passagework in the dominant key builds excitement. Then the first theme enters, a rocking, genuinely joyous tune in a choreographic mode that's nonetheless far too fast for dancing. To this Beethoven immediately adds a couple of excited wiggles, then another statement of the theme in the left hand, accompanied by broken octaves in the right hand, racing passagework over thunderous chords, and finally a strange, tolling theme, hammered out by both hands, followed at once by a Haydnesque variation of completely different character, a crisp and graceful right hand over a chattering left. Thus ends the first subject group. The second group begins in an easier, more lilting rhythm but is soon racing off in fast passagework, trills, and quick, bitten-off chords. In the brief development, a very beautiful passage, Beethoven places discrete thematic elements from the first and second groups into new combinations and minor keys, which offer a bit of welcome shade in this movement's headlong fury. Furthermore, as Rosen points out,[4] he keeps the volume down for the entire passage, short though it is. Beethoven begins the recapitulation with a glorious restatement of the first theme in a new sonority over racing sixteenth notes. The coda includes a reflective slow-down before the final, rattling rush to the closing chords.

An isolated work from 1814, the Sonata No. 27 in E Minor, Op. 90, has never been popular. The dichotomous nature of the two movements that make up the work is particularly striking: the opening section, austere, even stern in tone and structurally concentrated, is followed by a deeply lyrical rondo that seems poised between the melodic styles of Mozart and Schubert. Beethoven wrote the expression markings for this work, as he would for the next sonata, Op. 101, in German. In the

throes of a nationalism that turned its back on anything with the faint-
est whiff of Napoleon, Austrian musicians spurned the Corsican-born
conqueror's native language, Italian, which had of course been in wide
use among musical professionals for centuries.

In the first movement, which Beethoven marks to be played "with
animation, and with feeling and expression throughout," notice how
he presents the thematic elements individually, with only the thinnest
connections or even none at all; and how bare and unpadded everything sounds, sometimes painfully so. He begins with a stern tune of
somewhat folklike nature in a decisive, stamping rhythm. One hearing of the sonata will brand it into your mind; no other main theme
of Beethoven's is cut quite like this one. A mournful phrase replies,
followed by a spectral passage in rising octaves that leads to two sharp
chords in the rhythm of the opening then a falling scale, followed by
two milder-mannered versions of the chord and falling-scale passage.
The final element of the opening group is a powerful sequence built
on sharp chords in the right hand over a pulsing accompaniment in the
left that rise in volume, building to a naked, powerful dissonance and
preparing the way for the second subject, a long-spun, impassioned
melody over a rushing Alberti (broken-chord) pattern in the left hand,
followed by a thundering, rising octave figure in the left hand.

The development section, which is relatively long, begins with the
first theme played softly over the pulsing accompaniment. Soon the
second theme appears in the left hand under whirling figuration in the
right, and the composer, ending the passage in the most extraordinary
way, weaves the musical threads into two strands in an ever-tightening
canon, setting the stage for the return of the opening material. This
austere effect is striking when well played but can puzzle the first-time
listener. The brief coda, also remarkable for its lack of display, points
toward Beethoven's last style. The composer ends on a gently falling
phrase from the mournful second melodic element, with no flourish
or repeated chord: it's a remarkable finish, and one that hints at the
ending of the sonata.

"Not too fast, and very songfully played" is Beethoven's tempo
and expression indication for the long, elaborate, and very beautiful
rondo that concludes the work. It's in a cool E major that soothes the

ear after the asperities of the opening movement, and the main theme
of the rondo is luxuriously long and symmetrical above an easy, rocking accompaniment, in complete contrast with the breathless passion,
fragmented textures, and short, angular phrases of the first part. The
tune is highly memorable, like that of its opposite number in the first
movement, but in a distinctively singable way. Nor do the two episodes
disturb the steady, lyrical flow of Beethoven's conception. The first, a
floating idea in B major, is rhythmically derived from the main theme;
the second, while in a completely different rhythm (gentle quarter-
note chords over triplets), blends exquisitely into the overall flow. In
another interesting structural feature, Beethoven brings back the first
episode for an atypical appearance that expands this unusual rondo's
already generous proportions. And the coda, too, is ample. Beethoven
begins by fragmenting the theme but then brings it back for one final,
tender utterance. The astonishing final bars sound as though a new
discussion of the theme has begun. The voices rise, then fall, ending
the work on a conversational phrase in a quiet unison, with no chords
or hint of closing rhetoric: end of story. Beethoven moved more toward
this kind of understated conclusion—so different from the thunderous
codas of the middle period—in his later years, especially, as we'll see,
in the bagatelles. This may be his most restrained ending of all, and
it's perfectly suited to the profound lyricism of the work it rounds off.

The Sonata No. 28 in A Major, Op. 101, a great four-movement
work of 1816, closely anticipates Beethoven's final style, which would
soon emerge in its full splendor. But it can be a difficult piece to get
to know, seemingly disjunct in structure and just plain strange in a
couple of spots. The hard parts of Op. 101 sound like the reflections of
a musical intellect isolated by its lofty abstraction, comparable to many
moments in Bach's oeuvre. Luckily for the listener, though, the mood of
the work is upbeat, moving from tender in the beautiful opening movement to downright jolly in the finale; even the brief slow movement
seems to express an affect that's melancholy rather than tragic. What
can make Op. 101 hard to grasp are the dense, at times impenetrable
techniques Beethoven employs here. Don't be surprised if, as you listen
to Op. 101 over the years, there are periods where the textures seem
just too thick, or the composer's quick way of jumping between ideas

strikes you as peculiar. Beethoven's artistic judgment ultimately should prevail. Pianists also say that Op. 101 is also one of the toughest sonatas to play, as the composer himself acknowledged.[5]

Density of thought and texture and abrupt movement between ideas without transitional passages, for which Op. 101 is notable, are important characteristics of Beethoven's late style. Other late-period fingerprints include a finale-driven structure, in which the fourth movement is the longest and carries the sonata's greatest expressive weight, and a lavish use of counterpoint, especially in the second and fourth movements, as we'll see. Op. 101 is also interesting for having a "shadow" slow movement, rather than a fully developed one—a technique of Beethoven's middle and late periods, in which profound utterances in slow tempos are stated but never developed, being used instead as lead-ins to other movements, generally large-scale finales, as here. On the expressive side, the work is marked, especially in the first and third movements, by a rich lyricism that draws the listener in from the very first notes.

The opening movement is in sonata form, but Beethoven blurs the structural landmarks, presumably to deemphasize dramatic contrasts while enhancing the lyric flow of the music. Indeed, the ideas seem to sprout naturally one from the next; the movement develops more like a dialogue or conversation than a conflict. The relaxed, unemphatic tone that pervades this music is unusual for Beethoven, leading some critics to believe that the movement must have begun as one of the composer's improvisations at the keyboard. And this is true keyboard music, as the gorgeous, symmetrical tune that opens the work loops up the keyboard, then down in a graceful 6/8 rhythm, with the thumb lazily catching the bottom note of the phrase, sounding as though we have interrupted in mid-thought. Beethoven also achieves this effect by opening in the dominant key of E major, rather than A major, creating an atmosphere expectant and hovering rather than assertive, in the normal manner of sonata main themes; the composer also takes his time in reaching the nominal home key. An insinuating new four-note idea, almost speech-like in its directness, is replied to by its own mirror image, and the composer moves toward a sequence of broad, gently swaying chords, far off the beat. Syncopated chords continue to dominate the texture as the development begins in a slightly more urgent tone, with two measures even rising to *forte*—loud. The first theme is picked gently apart and recombined in new and lovely ways, the harmony remaining rich throughout. Yet the feeling of homecoming is powerful when it returns with ineffable sweetness in its original form, first in A minor, then in its nominal key, A major. Beethoven begins the coda with a massive, richly dissonant version of the swaying chord sequence that ended the exposition, then deploys the insinuating, eight-note theme again and again, clad in the richest harmonic garb, to conclude the movement ecstatically.

The spiky textures and aggressive rhythms of the proto-Schumannesque second-movement march contrast powerfully with the long, legato lines of the opening section. The march, in F major, an unusual key for a composition in A major, is in three parts, the explosive outer panels flanking a quiet and very strange middle section, with repeats adding length and weight. Wild indeed is the opening theme, which explodes in sharp accents, unconnected notes, and big leaps for both hands, but especially the left; it's immediately repeated. A second, related tune, which acts as a reply, takes us further afield harmonically as well as all over the keyboard. This section is marked by trills high in the treble, answered by grumbling figures in dotted (long-short) rhythm deep in the bass. Finally, Beethoven gathers the material rhythmically by means of unifying triplets in the left hand. The harmonies here are very bright, almost harsh. The middle section, which assumes the same role as the trio in a minuet you'd find in an earlier work, is a peculiar, crabbed canon (a strict form of contrapuntal writing) on a quiet and murmuring subject for two parts. It's really inexpressive and unconventional, so don't expect to appreciate it for quite a few listenings. Beethoven repeats its first part, then appends an even stranger canonic passage, which moves off, weirdly, in a different direction. A lengthy trill in the right hand begins the long path back to the march, which is played again from the beginning, but without any repeats.

Beethoven links the brief, slow third movement and the big finale that is the sonata's capstone. As noted, this is one of the master's "shadow" slow movements, a glorious lyric inspiration that does not receive full development, but acts as a prelude to another, bigger movement. (Another example of these is the brief, brooding slow movement that sets the stage for the finale of the String Quartet in C-sharp Minor, Op. 131.) Although less than a page long, this Adagio begins with a long-breathed melody in A minor. The opening musical paragraph, which reaches grandly to a high point in the sixth bar, ends in the eighth, giving way to a series of eloquent turns that pass from hand to hand. A sinking bass line leads to a more rapid movement, with the feel of a dying fall, similar to what you might hear at the end of a Chopin nocturne. A compression of harmony lets the listener know that something interesting is about to happen. A free cadenza follows, leading, unexpectedly for the first-time listener, to a repeat of the sweet opening four bars of the sonata. But an acceleration of its rhythm leads to a rushing scale and some excited trills, buzzing over athletically leaping chords. As we'll see, this is similar to what Beethoven does to begin the huge fugal finale of his next and biggest sonata, the "Hammerklavier," Op. 106. Then the cheerful first theme of the big sonata-form finale enters: a falling sequence in a sharp rhythm, followed by a four-note turn, presented contrapuntally. Though it opens with a big musical gesture, the final two chords of the phrase end tamely on fermatas. Beethoven's almost fugal presentation is significant: the theme is well suited to the full contrapuntal treatment Beethoven gives it in the development. The second part of the opening group is a more tranquil tune, presented over a fluid accompaniment. And a chunky rising-chord series, which will also end the movement neatly, followed by another interesting six-note idea in a rocking rhythm rounds out the first subject group. The much shorter second theme is a sunny, Schubertian duet for the right hand over a comical oom-pah-pah-pah rhythm in the left. The final idea of this fascinating parade of thematic characters is an energetic rhythmic figure, ripe with pauses and harmonic shifts.

Beethoven occupies the bulk of the long but fast-moving development with a fully developed three-voice fugue based on the first theme. It begins in the bass, continuing for a while in a grumbly low register. Beethoven's fugues are usually serious, but this one has a mechanistic, in-too-deep-to-quit feeling that makes it hard to tell whether the composer's tone is genuinely earnest or playfully mocking. But certainly for the player it's very serious business to learn and play clearly; the resemblance of this passage to the ferocious fugal finale of the "Hammerklavier" is striking. Finally the counterpoint gets very rough and choppy, and Beethoven decides to end it informally with a huge scale up the keyboard, ending in a straightforward statement of the main theme. If the tone of the fugue was ambiguously heroic, what follows is unmistakably comic as the theme runs itself out docilely on the four-note turns and the dainty fermatas; then the fugue revs up once again, but in reverse.

But the composer doesn't allow it much traction: instead, this being the recapitulation, he brings back the tranquil melody, now much welcomed by our counterpoint-saturated ears, trailed by all its fascinating kin. The coda begins with the energetic rhythmic figure deep in the bass. The falling opening figure interrupts. The fugue tries, amusingly, to get started one last time. But Beethoven rejects it, compressing his primary idea in its clearest form: the two falling notes followed by four. His piano writing here sparkles with pointillist sharpness and beauty. A trill low on the keyboard underlies nine tight repetitions of the main theme. And with a wave of his hand Beethoven dismisses the whole business with brisk, upward-rushing A major chords.

The "Hammerklavier" Sonata

Making the acquaintance of this, the longest, toughest, and most ambitious of the thirty-two sonatas, is an intimidating task. Yet every serious listener needs to undertake the project, and there is the absolute assurance that the climb to the peaks of the "Hammerklavier"—the Sonata No. 29 in B-flat Major, Op. 106—repays the effort: the view is sublime, and knowing the work will change you.

The menacing Teutonic nickname means only the inane "hammer-keyboard instrument." Still in the throes of the same anti-Napoleonic patriotism that inspired him to use German tempo indications exclusively in the Op. 90 sonata (see chapter 8, p. 98), the composer coined this term to avoid using the Italian words *piano* or *pianoforte*. But his insistence in these matters had begun to wane a bit. The Op. 101 sonata of 1816 was also conceived and published as "für das Hammerklavier," but that work contains tempo and expression marks in both German and Italian. There's so much mighty hammering in Op. 106 that the nickname fits this work better, impressionistically at least, than its mellow and cheerful predecessor, and it has stuck. The tempo markings of Op. 106 are, by the way, entirely and beautifully in Italian.

Beethoven began work on the "Hammerklavier" in 1817, wrestling with it over much of the following year. Upon its publication the sonata was greeted with respect and some incomprehension, fitting for music surpassing any work in the form in length, scope, and difficulty. But in a letter of 1819 to his pupil and assistant Ferdinand Ries, the master showed a curious indifference to the form in which it would be published in England. First offering to substitute another work altogether "should the Sonata not be suitable for London," Beethoven goes on to suggest three different formats, each one crippling to the vast sweep of the thing as he conceived it. Finally he writes, "I leave it to you to do as you think best."[1] The letter reveals the composer's urgent need for money in the age before copyright laws, a huge and time-consuming problem for Beethoven on which the big biographies are instructive. In any case, to most critics, the "Hammerklavier" Sonata is the landmark that opens Beethoven's late period. It was his first work on such a large a scale since the Seventh Symphony, of 1812, and its complexity and violence speak in a bold musical language that still sounds modern.

This ambitious composer's goals for the work were high: "I am writing a sonata now which is going to be my greatest," he told his pupil and friend Carl Czerny.[2] The character of the work's four huge movements fulfills his plan. It's exhilarating in the first movement, rough and weirdly comical in the scherzo. The third movement may be the grandest lament in Western music. And the huge fugal finale is an astonishing and terrifying discharge of power by contrapuntal means. The "Hammerklavier" is not charming, warm, or comforting, though catharsis may be found in Beethoven's artistic triumph there. The work chiefly blends epic and tragic modes of expression, and there is a feeling of an often violent exorcism. Again, Beethoven pitches the center of gravity of the "Hammerklavier" toward the massive finale, the densest movement in the work. But the heroic opening movement is a few bars longer, and the third movement is by far the longest in playing time.

From a technical standpoint, it's one of the composer's most extended experiments in the use of thirds as the crucial relationship between keys, the ultimate outcome of his harmonic experiments that began as early as the Variations in F Major, Op. 34 (see pp. 144–145), and the Sonatas Op. 31 No. 1 and Op. 53, "Waldstein" (see chapter 7). What this means to the listener is that the composer employs a harmonic pattern potentially longer and freer than that of the standard classical tonic-dominant, ultimately fraught with tension and conflict on a larger scale; but you have to hear it, as Beethoven uses it here, to grasp it. The discussion of keys may be a bit bewildering for a newbie, but it seems indispensable in the first movement to show precisely where and how Beethoven breaks the old rules and sets up a challenging, proto-modern harmonic system in their place. For pianists, it seems that the Himalayan Op. 106 will always be the ultimate interpretive challenge: "The combined musical and technical demands of this sonata make the most exacting of all tasks that a pianist can undertake," one respected survey of the keyboard literature flatly states.[3]

All the foregoing is unavoidably intimidating. Music from later in Beethoven's career sometimes presents even the most willing listener with backwardness and thorniness that seem nearly insurmountable. Other works that fall into this category are the Op. 101 sonata (which we looked at in the previous chapter), sections of the *Missa Solemnis*, and the String Quartet in B-flat Major, Op. 130, especially with the Great Fugue, Op. 133, as its colossal original finale. It's best to keep one's modesty in the presence of works like these: you may never learn to appreciate them—but then you may, unexpectedly, after years of listening in discomfort and bewilderment. Their knotty inwardness seems, again, to reflect the composer's profound isolation, both personal and intellectual: this is music for himself, which a small but ever-grateful band of initiates also grasps.

The flow of ideas in the first movement is overwhelming, and it moves at a brisk pace, so don't be surprised if you need to listen a few times just to get your bearings. Beethoven took his imperious opening idea from a fanfare he planned to use in a choral tribute to the Archduke Rudolph, "Vivat Rudolphus" (Long live Rudolph). It erupts from a low B-flat to a big, rattling chord sequence that holds the center and the upper keyboard, in the distinctive rhythm that dominates the movement; it's immediately repeated in a higher position. Its huge, treacherous leap speaks of the immense technical difficulties to come, and of the work's heaven-storming character. Moreover, inherent in the rhythm is a high-strung energy that sounds far better rendered by a pianist's hands and nervous system than any ensemble, instrumental or certainly vocal. Following a brief pause, the next thematic element enters. It's a melodious figure, more softly played, that soon comes to rest on a long pause, then starts up again in a more extended melodic strand. This soon leads to a new idea, detached but explosive chords similar in character to the opening phrase in the right hand, above shuddering, syncopations in the left. These quickly spread widely and grandly apart, leading to a restatement of the opening theme, first in B-flat major, then, surprisingly to the ear, in D major. Beethoven now moves to G major (a minor third down from the tonic key of B-flat major) for a long, gracefully winding phrase that prepares the way for the second subject.

The second theme group is another remarkable sequence. The thoughtful first idea, in G major, combines single notes and chords in a distinctive short-short-long-long rhythm before the next theme, sweeping figuration in the right hand over massive chords in the left. The effect is of gigantic breathing. This moves into yet another contrasting idea in a springing rhythm, then powerful chords and passagework that bring us to the closing idea, a beautiful, lyrical inspiration that opens with steady, singing chords in the right hand over triplets in the left; soon a long trill enters as a middle voice in the right hand, a stirring effect that's hard to play. This breaks into staccato chords over a rumbling bass, and Beethoven sets up the repeat by stating the rhythm of the opening theme in a simplified form; the exposition is repeated.

To blend the exposition and development, Beethoven picks up the staccato chords from the conclusion of the opening section but renders them more softly and playfully, also cleverly shifting the harmony from G major to E-flat major (a minor third down). Again using a stripped-down form of the opening rhythm, Beethoven initiates the powerful *fugato* (fuguelike) section that forms the heart of the development. Relentless in rhythm (long-short-short-long) and harmonically bold, it's also a murderous, finger- and arm-twisting passage marked by lots of fast double notes, hand-crossing, and big jumps. The passage is not a fugue, but rather a canon in four tightly woven parts. At last huge, leaping chords mark—at least temporarily—the cessation of counterpoint, and we find that Beethoven has reached B minor, the furthest key there is from the home tonality of B-flat major, reachable systematically only via his pattern of falling thirds; B minor is also a major third down from the E-flat of the preceding fugato, with the beautiful closing theme of the first subject group making an almost nocturne-like appearance now in B minor. He modulates easily to B major and then, in a swiftly rising sequence, across many keys. With a shout of triumph, the first theme returns in B-flat major in the right hand over a descending version of the *fugato* theme in the left: we have roamed far, but at last we have come to the recapitulation.

Beethoven's recapitulations almost always contain expansions of the original material, and this applies as well to as gigantic a work as the "Hammerklavier." Right away, for example, the second element of the first theme group receives a delicately phrased extension. And, now comfortably leaping between hostile keys, Beethoven plays the opening fanfare in B minor, moving easily back to B-flat major as though nothing had happened. The closing theme of the first group takes the stage one last time, marked again by its signature internal right-hand trill, as the powerful but strange coda begins. A long passage in chunky broken octaves kicks it off, leading to a cadenza-like phrase over huge trills in both hands, with unusual harmonic coloring and a pause on a dominant chord leading to scales. These wind up, as so much of this movement has, in an elemental version of the opening theme. A grumbling in remote harmony ("distant thunder")[4] appears deep in the bass, with the main theme in soft staccato above, but the last two chords are played loud, a fall in pitch accompanied by a jolting rise in volume. Finally, only falling quarter notes sound, alternating two soft with two loud, over the rumbling bass. Beethoven strips the opening theme down further, and the movement ends on a loud B-flat major chord and a bare B-flat in octaves.

Were it not part of this sonata, the scherzo might loom considerably larger in the structure of a different work. It is a sizable movement in every way, exciting and interesting on its own, but simply is the shortest section of this immense work. Sardonic in mood, the movement looks back to some of the scherzos of the big early sonatas, with those of Op. 2 No. 3 and Op. 7 as its models—although this is stranger than either. And its rough, Homeric humor might stand as a template for some of the *Diabelli Variations* (variation 5 or 7, for example), or a movement in one of the late string quartets.

The opening theme, a rising figure resembling that of the first movement, is a fast but still lilting satire of a minuet into which Beethoven introduces odd changes of harmony. Chains of falling thirds, here an open part of the right-hand part, again characterize the musical texture. A trio in B-flat minor billows menacingly but beautifully, with little preparation. This is a direct descendant of the trios from the early sonatas mentioned above, with the melody emerging above fast triplets; it also has a melodic swing very close to that of the main theme of the first movement of the "Eroica" Symphony. Here, Beethoven passes it easily from right hand to left and back again.

But the next passage, a kind of second trio, is really odd: the tune sounds like an infantile schoolyard taunt, pecked out in individual notes, then harmonized with appropriate petulance. An angry falling passage leads to a huge, sweeping, scale up the keyboard and a chuckling dominant chord, played *tremolando*; then the first theme returns, with a slightly more elaborate accompaniment. But again, Beethoven holds a surprise: another furious outburst, this in the form of fifteen banged-out, repeated Bs, followed by a B-flat and a final escape of the lilting minuet theme, high on the keyboard. As in the first movement, the composer focuses on the tension between the two tones of B-flat and B-natural: there he does it structurally, while here he puts them in direct and brutal conflict.

The Adagio sostenuto that follows is one of the greatest slow movements ever written. It's a lament laid out by Beethoven on the grandest scale, speaking in tragic accents, with little conventional consolation to be found in its vast length and breadth. Listening to this tragic revelation by the mature composer at the peak of his powers must needs be a moving and sorrowful moment. Be prepared to give it the time and attention it demands: its playing time can range from just over seventeen minutes, as in Richard Goode's recording of the sonata, to 22:20 in Solomon's—both outstanding performances. Its message may be filled with pain, but the novice listener can approach the Adagio knowing that it is in a straightforward sonata form, its themes well delineated and easy to recognize.

In addition to the tempo marking, Beethoven gives the beautiful expression mark *Appassionato e con molto sentimento* (no translation necessary, and thank goodness he went back to using Italian!) The opening bar of the movement acts as a lead-in, and is perhaps the most inspired late addition to a work in musical history. Beethoven decided to insert the two rising notes that make up the opening measure after the publisher had sent him proofs of the sonata. What this brief rising figure accomplishes is enormous, bridging the wide harmonic gap between the B-flat major of the Scherzo and the F-sharp minor of the Adagio and giving the slow movement a rising opening figure, like all the others in the sonata. And its solemnity complements the character of the grand melody it introduces. That colossal, hymnlike main theme rises and falls majestically for twenty-five extraordinary measures; its character is as sorrowful as it seems possible for music—or any art—to express. At two points, the line breaks free from the thick chordal texture to rise up alone, but it stays aloft for only two measures. Yet despite its tragic character, the 6/8 rhythm remains fluid, and the melody moves freely, with Beethoven allowing it to float up, though sorrowfully, again, at the end of its vast cycle. After a pause, the next thematic element enters grandly, like a new character in a drama. Over the powerful throb of the left-hand accompaniment and marked *con grand'espressione*, the right hand comes in with a despairing, operatically styled melody that is nonetheless purely pianistic in its layout, with multiple parts sounding, opulently, at once. By far the grandest of Beethoven's operatically inspired passages for piano, this at last compares with what Chopin would later achieve in a similar idiom, in which the composers use the resources of the piano to pay homage to the direct, impassioned Italian vocal style (although a passage in Op. 110 is equally wonderful; see pp. 126–127). This magnificent phrase leads into a complex passage of winding sixteenth notes in dominant harmony, setting the stage for the second subject group.

Initially in D major, and contrasting with the first subject group in its otherworldly affect, the second thematic complex opens with a broad idea, in which the right hand crosses over, first tolling deep in the bass, with the same phrase then played in octaves high on the keyboard, the left playing a continuous murmuring accompaniment. This moves into a more flowing passage for both hands, which leads to a final idea, a profound sequence of rocking chords in a broader harmony that seems the movement's climax, a transcendent experience finding expression.

The brief development does what development sections do, taking the material presented and moving it around in a deeply lyrical discussion. And with such extraordinary material, the passage is of surpassing beauty. Beethoven's chief strategy is to render the hymnlike first

theme of the first group in broken phrases and repeated over a surging left-hand accompaniment, in a rainbow of dark tonalities. Finally
the sequence starts to fall on a limping rhythm, which leads into the
recapitulation.

Here Beethoven gives the hymnlike theme to steady chords in the
left hand, under a dark, lavishly billowing ornamentation in the right,
the affect is of the most passionate despair imaginable. The grandiose
operatic theme—again, *con grand' espressione*—recurs, even more
richly decorated and even more abandoned in its own outpouring of
sorrow, as does the more calm and distant second subject group. And
again, the profound closing idea seems to reach a new plane of thought.
But this also signals the start of the long, majestic coda. This magnificent passage, so substantial as to seem like a second development, opens
with the first theme, in compressed form, followed by the tolling of
the first theme of the second group. But this grows uncharacteristically
agitated, leading to hammered notes in the right hand over *tremolandi*
in the left. The hymnlike theme comes back again, at greater length,
followed by the operatic theme, marked by a passionate and despairing run in the right hand. Again the dark hymn returns, followed by
immense F-sharp major chords that close the movement. The move into
the major key only adds to the movement's incantatory tragic power.

Because the finale proper is a huge, fast, dense, sometimes violent
fugue, nearly four hundred bars long and occupying ten minutes' playing time, Beethoven knew that to break the nocturnal magic of his
twenty-minute Adagio and jump directly into the turbulent fugue would
be an aesthetic catastrophe. So he wrote a remarkable quasi-improvised
introduction, fully three minutes long, to bridge the gap. In addition
to shifting the mood from dreamlike to energetic, it also introduces
counterpoint as the topic of the finale, at the same time moving the
key between the remote F-sharp minor of the Adagio and the finale's
B-flat major. This passage, which is in the slow tempo *largo*, opens with
single, delicate Fs that rise up swiftly across the keyboard, followed by
sinking notes in the left hand and chords in gently wavering harmony in
the right. Suddenly, a phrase in falling three-voice counterpoint enters
hesitantly, then halts gracefully. More falling notes in the left hand and
chords in the right give way to a passage reminiscent of one of Bach's

two-part inventions, though Beethoven puts this phrase in a remote and shocking B major. More gentle chords ensue, followed by a busy, recherché copy of Bach's fiery keyboard style. But this, too, pauses; more chords now lead to falling, cadenza-like scales, with an excited trill at the bottom, which leads into a powerfully rhythmic phrase that begins quietly but quickly builds to a seething boil. Now fully alert and tense with anticipation, the listener's mind is ready for the fugue.

If you've never heard the "Hammerklavier" finale before, it's crucial for you to understand that the overall character of the movement is aggressive, even violent in spots and that its contrapuntal textures bristle with difficulty. Beethoven did not write this movement to please the listener's ear, but rather to assert his mastery over the many fugal processes he uses and to bring the colossal tensions already generated in the sonata to an even higher level, then to relieve them somewhat (although he does not provide the same kind of dramatic, cathartic release at the end as he does in the big middle-period sonatas, especially the "Waldstein" and the "Appassionata"). Also, because it's a fugue, the movement is inevitably more intellectually driven; so while its three subjects are strong in character, their development is guided by contrapuntal logic, rather than by the drama of sonata form. So prepare to be challenged by the difficulty of the music. In fact, don't be surprised if its dense fury puts you off for a while: Beethoven didn't intend that the fugue be loved, but rather that it be listened to in awe.

The tempo is *allegro risoluto*, with the modifier meaning "resolute." Rising trills in the right hand over proud, pouncing chords in the left recall the lead-in to the finale of Op. 101; there's some final, excited scurrying among some scales and chords as the musical lines bustle to their places and the first subject enters. A low note bounces up to a long trill; it's followed by a couple of falling scales, then a long passage of scurrying sixteenth notes. (Trills have a crucial and persistent thematic rather than decorative place in this movement and are rarely out of the picture.) After a few bars, the subject enters again above the running notes. Almost immediately, the second subject, which also begins with a rising bounce before a more flowing profile in eighth notes, enters in the left hand. This easily recognized subject also plays a big role over the course of the movement. And soon another subject, also in eighth notes and starting on a more gently rising sequence, enters the scene. The texture is already as active and as challenging to the player and listener as one could imagine, and the fugue has just begun. A slightly more lyrical, upward-reaching passage can be heard as Beethoven moves into G-flat major, but it's brief, for it serves only to introduce the first of the movement's big contrapuntal displays. This one is *augmentation*, in which the time value of the notes is lengthened. Because of the distortion of the notes, the subjects are difficult to pick out here. You'll hear a very long trill in the right hand, followed by a lot of long, syncopated notes and the second subject banging furiously about in the left hand, then a long sequence of trills for both hands in a strange harmonic garb. This gives way to the more lyrical, upward-reaching phrase, now in A-flat major.

Next in Beethoven's armory is the *retrograde* episode, where the theme is presented backward. Here the fugue seems to hesitate, as the runs we've grown used to hearing move downward go up instead. Trills also play a big role in this passage, which is actually one of the more lyrical in the movement, though still hard to grasp. Then follows the *inversion*, where the subject is turned upside down, so that an interval that rose in its original form falls instead. But at least here and in the retrograde episode the themes are still recognizable. Trills now dominate the texture, as Beethoven builds the counterpoint to a really violent climax, ending on snarling trills, falling octaves, and sharp, detached chords, followed by a long, deliberate pause. In the midst of his contrapuntal battles, Beethoven provides a moment of repose in the form of another three-voice fugue on a suave new subject in D major, played legato and reminiscent of Bach in a sacred mood. It may be less than a minute long, but it's a genuinely welcome relief for most mortals. Beethoven's modulation back to B-flat major at the end of the passage is smooth and quiet, too, and of startling beauty.

We may, indeed, feel flung back into the fray as the familiar subjects start up their furious activity again. Beethoven has two more important contrapuntal displays up his sleeve, the first a combination of the first and third subjects, and then a grandiose *stretto*, a device whereby subjects enter in close succession, before the full statement of the subject has ended, creating a sense of contrapuntal climax. But even here

Beethoven moves at full speed, without sentimentalizing the capstone of his fugue. Two short but decisive dominant-and-tonic chords signal the end of the contrapuntal development and the start of the coda, massive and potent as befits a work of this size and scope. After opening with trills in an unusual harmonic guise, Beethoven then gives an immense trill to the left hand, down near the bottom of the keyboard, over which a huge scale rises over a span of three bars. The trill rumbles along as fragments of several of the movement's many themes pass above. Finally, Beethoven slows the tempo very considerably to *poco adagio* for three more weird trills, leading into a cadence that shifts softly but mightily into place on the expectant (dominant seventh) chord. The falling scales of the main subject come back in a final furious incarnation as trills injecting nervous energy and chords carry the tonal banner a couple of peaks higher than we ever imagined, and on to the final cadence of four massive chords. A crucial detail is how Beethoven places the final two chords, which are normally the listener's great release, on syncopated beats, rather than firmly on the bar line, thus maintaining tension to the very end—and beyond.

The Final Trilogy

The last three sonatas—the E major, Op. 109; the A-flat major, Op. 110; and the C minor, Op. 111—are objects of fully justified reverence. They stand alongside Beethoven's late string quartets, the Ninth Symphony, and the *Diabelli Variations* as the peaks of his third-period instrumental masterworks; but so much has been bruited about their mystical qualities that some first-timers may be intimidated by them even before actually hearing the music. But unlike Opp. 101 and 106, Beethoven does not use them as testing grounds for challenging musical and pianistic problems. All the advanced mechanical means and the hard-won wisdom of his late style blend joyfully in these sonatas to serve comprehensible expressive ends; form and content meet more happily, and all three are easier to play and, probably, to grasp, than Opp. 101 and 106—which is not to suggest that there's anything simple about these intense, complex, profound works. And while their spirituality, particularly that of Op. 111, may be undeniable, this rich, openly emotional music is eminently accessible to the open-minded listener.

That these advanced works were initially greeted with bafflement and rarely performed comes as no surprise. Only the most serious pianists of the nineteenth and early twentieth centuries, such as Hans von Bülow,[1] Anton Rubinstein,[2] and presumably Ferruccio Busoni, performed them. Artur Schnabel was their chief advocate afterward, and a persuasive one. One of his programs consisted of two valedictory sonatas: Schubert's B-flat Major, D. 959, as the opening half and Beethoven's Op. 111 after the intermission; a simpler, bolder, and more sublime program cannot be imagined. Schnabel's recital, while

immensely challenging to himself and his audience, offered by way
of balance the differences of style and structure of the two masters.
Schnabel's approach also served to emphasize the faraway conclusion of
Op. 111, which is surely hard to follow. Busoni's intellectual pupil Egon
Petri played all three in a 1954 recital that was recorded, opening with
Op. 81a for good measure. But the equally respected Romanian-born
pianist Clara Haskil placed Op. 111 at the end of the first half of a 1953
recital program, preceded by Bach's E Minor Toccata and three sonatas
by Scarlatti; the second half of her serious, sophisticated, and beautifully performed program (also recorded) consisted of Schumann's *Abegg
Variations*, two Debussy etudes, and Ravel's Sonatina. The Beethoven
doesn't suffer for being in such varied company.

It's now common for Beethoven's final three to be played as a single
recital program, with Opp. 109 and 110 before and Op. 111 after the
intermission; Rudolf Serkin did so, as has Mitsuko Uchida. It may be
too much of a good thing, in its late-Beethoven way, for some listeners
to have to hear all three together, no matter how well played, because
each sonata has so much to offer the attentive listener on its own, and
because each speaks so personally to everyone. And it may be, too, that,
as indisputably great as these final three are, they now, along with the
"Waldstein," the "Appassionata," and the "Hammerklavier," dominate
the recital stage to the disadvantage of other Beethoven sonatas.

The most notable structural tendency of the final three sonatas is
Beethoven's continual emphasis, already so pronounced in Opp. 101 and
106, on the finale. The theme and variations that concludes Op. 109
is almost three times as long as the two movements that precede it put
together, while that of Op. 110 is a bold formal experiment that fuses
the arialike lament of the third movement with the rising sap of the
fugue that is the fourth. The eighteen-minute journey to the far reaches
of the spirit that concludes Op. 111 is surely in its own league, even in
Beethoven's output; it's twice the length of the stormy opening movement, as well as its complement and resolution. While the composer
does not call the finale of Op. 111 a theme and variations, that's the
form most performers and listeners perceive for it. In any case, a greater
reliance on variation form, where everything springs from one thematic

idea, is another crucial element of Beethoven's late style. Others characteristics include an extreme harmonic density and richness and a lack of rhetorical flourishes, alongside a boldness and freedom in moving between ideas. There are some curious sonorities, too, including some the occasional thick keyboard writing of a type we've heard before, and moments where the hands play far apart, creating the strange but very characteristic late Beethoven sound of high and low notes sounded at the same time. And, while Beethoven shows plenty of his old fighting spirit in all three works, especially the opening movement of Op. 111, there is also peculiar to them a sweet, milky mildness that he finds in himself and expresses in his music late in his life, impossible to miss, and infinitely touching to hear.

Beethoven composed the Sonata No. 30 in E Major, Op. 109, in 1820; it was published the following year. Of the last three sonatas, it is richer and more fantastical than the other two, which are more contained, in their fashion. The three movements of Op. 109 differ radically from each other in character. The opening movement, which runs about four minutes, is profoundly lyrical. The quick (two minutes plus) second movement is fleet-footed and somewhat like a bagatelle, though more tightly structured. Both movements do, however, offer a sense that the composer is pressing ahead, rather than developing his themes in some traditional, sonata-like way; Beethoven clearly intended both to act as preludes to the climactic third movement. That third movement, a theme and six variations, far outweighs the opening two sections—twelve to fourteen minutes' playing time for it seems typical. Deliberate and self-referential like all variations, the finale is utterly different in character and scope from and yet paradoxically acts as the culmination of the opening movements, answering the questions they pose.

The short, dense opening movement begins directly with a sweet melody in the middle of the keyboard that seems to burst like bubbles, and in which the action of the left hand echoes that of the right. Like all of the three contrasting ideas of which the movement is built, it has an improvisational feel. The tune also bears a superficial resemblance to that of the finale of the G Major Sonata, Op. 79, but is far richer harmonically and emotionally than that charming trifle. Beethoven's tempo marking for the movement is *vivace, ma non troppo*: lively, but not too much so. But the opening theme is only seconds long before the composer breaks off into the second theme, a magnificent, richly ornamented passage in a much slower tempo that sweeps grandly over the keyboard and between keys before leading back to the opening theme; this Beethoven now unfolds at greater length and dynamic range, giving full rein to its ecstatic emotion. The second, slower passage returns, followed by a brief reprise of the opening theme. The third theme, a lovely sequence of thoughtful, plain chords that contrasts texturally with the other themes, interrupts to be heard just this once. Then the opening idea returns to end this highly compressed sonata movement that seems to have little of the conventional about it. The frequent and sudden changes Beethoven imposes on the music will strike the first-time listener—just as it does one who has known it for decades—with an improvisatory quality; but of course it is exquisitely and densely wrought.

More uniform in speed and texture, the second movement is hardly begun before it's over. Marked *prestissimo* (very quick), it opens with a brave, almost thunderous musical gesture in the left hand but soon melts to a softer dynamic level and a gentler, more lilting melodic mode of expression. A grumbling theme is heard in the bass; thematic fragments appear here and there in incarnations that are alternately plaintive and aggressive. A chord sequence at the center offers contrast, if not real repose, before the opening theme returns. Unlike in the first movement, all the material here is similar in character. And Beethoven ends the movement as he began it, with big gestures: a furious scale that seems spat out and a closing sequence of sharp chords. Here we have the angry, impetuous Beethoven we know well, but there's unease and melancholy in this music, as well. If more delicate in texture, the music is even more compressed structurally than in the opening movement, and just as carefully assembled. It is, in its way, every bit as fantastical, but here the composer expresses more troubled emotion. It may go by in a flash, but there is much to take in.

In the finale, a noble, memorable, and richly melodic theme is followed by six variations of radically different character—some containing dramatic alterations of speed and texture within themselves. A reiteration of the theme then ends the movement. If you have heard Bach's

Goldberg Variations, you will recognize that this is the same structure, in a smaller package. Bach's masterwork must have been on Beethoven's mind as he wrote this great movement, in which high fantasy, colossal compositional technique, including some thick counterpoint, and an undeniable spiritual element combine. The movement stands alongside the *Diabelli Variations* as Beethoven's two grand tributes to Bach's work.

Like Bach's theme for the *Goldberg Variations*, Beethoven's for this movement is sixteen measures long. Bach's theme is complex and dance-like; Beethoven's sounds more like a song or perhaps a hymn. Like the earlier master's theme, Beethoven's is in two eight-bar phrases, which are repeated. Beethoven feels the need to return to two languages for his tempo and expression marks, at least at the beginning: *Gesangvoll, mit innigster Empfindung* (songful, with inmost, or deepest, expression) is his beautiful German direction; *andante molto cantabile ed espressivo* (flowing and very songlike and expressive) is the fairly comparable Italian. These speak clearly to the nature of the theme as it rises and falls, reaching for its tranquil, heartfelt closing cadence.

The first variation, marked *molto espressivo*, is a slow waltz that seems to look ahead to Chopin in the richness of its ornamentation over a rock-steady waltz beat. But there is something of the aria about it, too, as though a great soprano has embellished the tune. When you listen, pay attention to the repeated high notes preceded by a grace note, a very operatic-sounding alteration of the melodic line. The harmony beneath is extremely rich throughout.

A combination of touch and keyboard texture marks the second variation, which opens with the melody broken into single notes taken between the hands, marked *leggiermente*—lightly. But the pointillist sound quickly gives way to the melody, played in repeated, sustained notes in the right hand over thick chords in the left, the entire passage marked *teneramente*—held. As the variation progresses, the pointillist phrasing takes on more weight, and the passage ends with some thick chords in the left hand. But the mood is blissful, and the sound, feeling, and keyboard writing look back to the first movement.

Only seconds long, the third variation races ahead in *fugato*, with Beethoven employing contrapuntal techniques without taking on the responsibilities of a complete fugue. Spirits are high as it moves without pause into the fourth variation. This slower, very complex passage combines and contrasts two ideas, the first a languid, barcarolle-like idea in which the melody is stretched out into long, graceful phrases; in the second it is transformed into a strange, pulsing idea above which one four-note phrase hovers, at once ecstatically and humorously.

The jovial mood and thick counterpoint of variation 5 are quite reminiscent of some of Bach's *Goldberg Variations*. The climactic sixth variation begins with the melody held to lower and middle voices, where it seems to struggle against the repeated notes accompanying it. As the section progresses, Beethoven loosens the rhythm and speeds the accompaniment to quicker notes and finally to blazing trills in both hands. As the theme reaches its second half (the eighth bar of its original form), Beethoven sets it free in a torrent of passagework in the right hand over a trill deep in the bass; in the final phrase the tune is locked into a series of short, detached notes high on the keyboard. The effect is like that of a frozen stream melting into glorious, free movement, and the exaltation it conveys is unmistakable. To conclude the movement, the theme is repeated in all its beauty, and now with our added wonderment at all Beethoven mined from it.

A profound lyricism pervades the Sonata No. 31 in A-flat Major, Op. 110, composed in 1821 and 1822 and published in the latter year. This quality is evident from start to finish in all but the second movement, making Op. 110 probably the best-known and best loved of the final trilogy; it can be heard in its entirety on tracks 6, 7, and 8 of the CD that accompanies this book. Beethoven began the sonata while ill, late in 1821, recovering as the year ended. Op. 110 seems to track a parallel course from muted sadness to a newfound strength and joy. Indeed, while the lyrical nature of the work is clear and the triumph of lyricism at the sonata's end complete and glorious, the sensitive listener may hear that it's struggling almost continually to break through a containment that verges on weariness in the first movement and sorrow in the third. Moreover, the third and fourth movements, as noted above, are inextricably merged in one of Beethoven's most remarkable structural experiments, where the composer combines elements of vocal and instrumental music and employs the contrasting baroque techniques of aria and fugue to achieve his expressive goals.

An argument might be made that the Sonata No. 13 in E-flat Major, Op. 27 No. 1—the first *Sonata quasi una fantasia* of 1801—is a forerunner of this penultimate sonata, particularly the fused third and fourth movements, the former styled as an aria, the latter a fugue. The fugue in the finale of the Op. 101 sonata (see pp. 100–104) also offers some precedent.

Moderato cantabile molto espressivo is Beethoven's tempo indication for the magical opening movement of Op. 110; he amplifies this with the Italian *con amabilità* (amiably) and, in parentheses, the German word *sanft* (gentle), creating a nearly Shakespearean stage direction. The movement is fascinating structurally for having only one theme (or thematic group) but a well-defined development section. In it Beethoven exploits the frictions within the thematic group, which turn out to be considerable, given the gentle sound and contained nature of the musical ideas. There is no loud playing called for in this movement, which offers a sense that the composer is holding his musical thought and emotion under closest rein.

The main theme combines melodies and fragments into a rich whole that combines a range of melodic, rhythmic, and harmonic ideas. The opening one, three and a half measures long, seems dancelike in nature, pausing on a graceful trill (CD Track 6, 0:12); then at 0:16 launching into a soaring, single-note, vocally styled melody over a homophonic accompaniment in the left hand that represents a late flowering of Beethoven's most fundamental classical instincts. This breaks apart into ecstatic arpeggios (0:38) that are keyboard writing at its purest, followed by melting transitional passages, beginning at 0:59, above trills (1:16) that seem to be struggling to express themselves fervently; one where the hands play widely separated (1:32); a big falling scale (1:40); and finally a temporizing phrase of sixteenth notes in the right hand, wandering amiably above rich chords in the left (1:51).

Next, Beethoven begins the short but remarkable development section (2:08), putting the graceful opening phrase through eight exquisite but crushingly dark harmonic excursions before guiding it back to A-flat major. The recapitulation of the opening is played ecstatically above a fluttering thirty-second-note arpeggiated figuration (2:56) that combines two thematic and textural elements. Finally the dance seems to win out, and the opening theme sounds chastely in the left hand (3:08) like a horn call in a ballet score; the songlike melody returns (3:16).

Next (3:28–3:35) Beethoven puts the theme through a profound harmonic shift, moving from A-flat major to the remote key of E major. This is what's known as an *enharmonic* alteration, where the composer exploits the dual nature of a note, in this case A-flat/G-sharp, to jump a tremendous harmonic distance. The maneuver looks dry described on paper, but when you hear the music, you feel the shift seismically, to the tips of your toes. Schubert did it often, as did Chopin; the enharmonic alteration sounds most potent at the hush of low volume, as Beethoven does it here. Yet, having forced his way from A-flat major to E major, Beethoven stays there only briefly, revealing the arpeggiated figure in the new tonality and then the melting transitional passage before pushing back into A-flat major (3.59). He repeats the melodies that struggle to rise, then the opening phrase, then the temporizing phrase that wanders about.

A calm passage in which chords seem to seek level ground rhythmically and harmonically (5:16) opens the short but fantastically beautiful coda. First (5:33) we hear the arpeggiated figure, then, in the left hand at 5:54, the opening phrase, tenderly decorated by notes in the right. One bar of more serious chords presents a threat of a threat, but Beethoven lightens the texture for the closing.

The vehement two-minute second movement needs no more than one attentive listening for it to be imprinted on one's memory. In it we hear the aggressive Beethoven we know well from so many driving scherzo movements. But the difference in tone and texture between this movement and the rest of the sonata is marked: all the phrases are even in length, and most of them are repeated. The form of the movement is that of a quick German dance, with a falling figure in the right hand over a rising one in the left. The opening phrase, played softly, has an almost childlike plainness (CD Track 7); it's answered by a loud, violent phrase that moves downward (0:02), and the entire tune has a strongly memorable cut.

The second (0:08) opens with a boisterous phrase, followed by a quieter one, then a carefully calculated ritardando (0:21) followed by a two-bar rest (0:24), then an explosive closing cadence; all the opening sections are repeated. The middle section offers a lightening of texture and rhythm, if not a change in the rather fierce tone, as the left hand spins out a wild, fiddly, falling figure (0:43) in the right hand over individual notes struck on the off-beats in the left. Beethoven then reprises the opening phrase (1:12), building in another interesting slowdown at 1:20, but instead of ending on a closed cadence, he begins the coda at 1:57 with crashing chords that modulate away from F minor to F major, finally (2:03) breaking one chord in the left hand under the long one struck in the right; his purpose is to clear the way for the change of tone and structure of the combined slow movement and fugal finale. This scherzo is rougher than its opposite number in Op. 109; Op. 111 has no room in its scheme for a quick movement like these.

     I. Recitativo (CD Track 8, 0:40)
    II. Klagender Gesang/Arioso Dolente (sorrowful aria) (1:42)
   III. Fuga (3:35)
   IV. L'istesso tempo di Arioso (the same tempo as the aria) (5:52)
    V. L'istesso tempo della Fuga poi a poi di nuovo vivente (the same tempo as the fugue, bit by bit growing more lively) (8:31)
 [VI. nonfugal apotheosis of fugue theme and coda] (9:35)

These six sections, including an unofficial one to describe the closing bars, show the large, complex structure of the combined slow movement and finale. The *recitativo* with which the sequence begins is an instrumental interpretation of a vocal style that comes from opera or church music, such as cantata or oratorio. In a recitative, text is musically declaimed—"recited"—so that it can be heard clearly. Since this sonata is an instrumental work, Beethoven's *recitativo* is obviously a fantasy based on vocal music; but also a style he used before, as, for example, in the opening movement of the D Minor Sonata, Op. 31 No. 2. This eloquent *recitativo* opens in a slow tempo with chords that, however, range swiftly over wide harmonies. Falling speechlike patterns (0:40–1:42) pull with the inexorability of gravity toward the body of the slow movement itself, which the composer labels Adagio ma non troppo and places in throbbing chords (1:42) in the exceedingly rare key of A-flat minor.

Above, the melody enters (1:50) in a passionate, sinuous line, styled like a despairing melody from Italian opera. In the score, the composer calls this the *Klagender Gesang*, then beneath that, in Italian, *Arioso dolente*. The German has the more straightforward meaning: mournful song. The Italian term reverberates with complexity: *arioso* has four very similar meanings in the *Oxford Dictionary of Music*, but it's basically a short, melodious passage, like this one; it does not, perhaps, do justice to the breadth of Beethoven's long-spun melody. (*Dolente* means doleful or sorrowful.) Beethoven's pattern does not allow for repetition of phrases; the tune reaches up to series of climactic high notes (2:26) that would do Bellini, the master of *bel canto* opera, proud. Finally the melody falls, tangled in the darkest harmonies of the accompaniment, and comes to rest on a somber cadential phrase deep in the bass (3:22).

The three-part fugue begins without pause, quietly, in A-flat major, its gently rising and falling, highly memorable subject (3:35) outlining the primal-sounding interval of a fourth. The 6/8 time in which Beethoven sets the fugue into offers much flexibility in the rhythmic expression of his counterpoint but is above all lilting and lyrical. It shows his intimate knowledge of Bach, who often used the same fluid time signature in his own fugues. The second voice enters four bars later above the first (3:41) as the first turns into a gently flowing middle voice; the third voice comes in closely and mellifluously above the second (3:50). A trill (4:03) signals a new textural openness and joy as Beethoven hammers out the fugue subject grandly in octaves in the bass. He then closes his textures up a bit, working in tighter counterpoint, with passages in chromatic harmony and the flowing middle voice dominating the rhythm. Finally, the theme appears in one particularly memorable incarnation (5:22) in the left hand. This part writing gives off a gentle glow throughout, at no point resembling the spiky contrapuntal styles of Op. 101 or the "Hammerklavier."

But the joy and richness of the fugal development wilts after a sequence of diminished chords and arpeggios, followed by a G minor chord (5:52) and a return of the throbbing accompaniment of the *arioso dolente* (5:58). Here Beethoven breaks his long, mournful melody into short fragments that seem to be gasping for breath. Indeed, his expressive markings tell the story: *Ermattet, klagend*, meaning exhausted, and, of course, mournful, in German; then *perdendo le forze, dolente* in Italian. The former phrase means "losing strength." And indeed the pauses Beethoven works in between the notes suggest exhaustion, despair, and sobbing. In this sense there's another aspect to Beethoven's art: he seems to be imitating baroque masters: Beethoven's broken, weeping phrasing seems as though it might have been modeled directly on a passage from an aria of Bach or Handel in which despair is the ruling affect and weeping is imitated by the broken melodic line; furthermore, the key is G minor, very common in the baroque. And as Charles Rosen points out,[3] that key sits immediately "below" A-flat major, giving it a depressed sound in the tonal context of this sonata. The *arioso* moves as before to the somber phrase that closed the passage the first time around (7:54), but after that Beethoven adds ten terrifying repeated G major chords (8:00) of suffocating weight, deep in the keyboard, followed by an eleventh broken chord that creeps up the keyboard (8:22).

This alarming passage leads directly into the final appearance of the fugue subject (8:31), which Beethoven reintroduces in inversion, meaning that the notes go down where they originally went up. It's worth noting that his expression markings in Italian and German call for "bit by bit returning to new life." He also, as at 8:56 and 9:21, indulges in the fugal technique of *diminution*, which, by quickening the notes of the theme, tightens up the contrapuntal gears and raises the temperature of the music, at the same time sounding like an embellishment. Suddenly the subject is thundered out in the bass over rattling sixteenth notes in the right hand (9:35); Beethoven has passed through the fugue to an apotheosis of its theme. Now the right hand sings out the final phrase of the fugue subject, over and over, highlighted by harmonic shadings that are as various as they are glorious; then he goes once more through the full fugue subject, now richly harmonized, as the left hand continues with its ecstatic fast accompaniment. The excitement mounts to a level we have not heard before in this work as it rushes to a brilliant ending on an A-flat major arpeggio and a single closing chord that seems heart-felt, hard-won, yet not in the least showy.

Writing about music should to stay close to the subject, avoid extramusical comparisons, and, above all, not gush. But a work as utterly great, wonderful, and life-changing as Beethoven's final piano sonata, No. 32 in C Minor, Op. 111, published in 1823, make these rules difficult, if not impossible, to obey. Part of the difficulty of steering clear of outside associations may be ascribed to the clear structural connection between the two movements, the stormy opening contrasting so vividly with, yet paradoxically setting the stage for, the meditations and ecstasies of the second. The astonishing five-page description of Op. 111 in chapter 7 of Thomas Mann's 1947 novel *Doktor Faustus* is a perfect example of the subjective flights of fancy to which the work can drive a sensitive listener, for better or worse. Mann's exegesis seems packed equally with gems of insight and twaddle, but it's surely a heartfelt tribute, and fun to read.

Op. 111 unquestionably forms a cohesive spiritual, though not a narrative, whole from start to finish. It is also the finest farewell imaginable by Beethoven to the piano sonata, which, like all its siblings, is completely individual in form and thought. And finally, it's an adieu to his signature key of C minor, which he puts through its final, fierce paces before finding in it a C major resolution far different and—to those who know it—incomparably more heroic than any of his middle-period finales. The comfort Op. 111 offers seems different in kind and far deeper than the thunderous victory of, say, the "Waldstein" Sonata.

The two-movement form for Op. 111 is written in stone: there's no room for a scherzo or a triumphant finale. The conflict of the sonata-form-with-introduction first movement finding resolution in the ineffable theme and variations of the second is one of Beethoven's keenest inspirations—you have to hear it to understand, but one hearing will clear that question up, at least. But Op. 111 isn't an easy piece, at least for the first few hearings, so be patient. The opening movement, at least, should make some sense from the start.

The first movement's complex three-part structure opens with a weighty introduction. Beethoven follows this with the main body of the movement, in sonata form with heavy contrapuntal inflections, and ends the movement with a short coda of striking new material. The composer signals his high intentions with a sixteen-bar introduction of immense force and gravity, an epic utterance. Instead of a more standard tempo indication, he places the unusually suggestive *maestoso*—majestic—at the top. *Maestoso* is more commonly given as a modifier, as in *allegro maestoso*, but here the composer is offering clear guidance to player and listener as to the nature of the passage.

The fiercest dissonance in the sharpest rhythm opens the piece, followed by trills, chords, and flourishes that are grander than grand—*maestoso*, indeed. Beethoven repeats this craggy idea twice, each time at a higher pitch, then moves to a phrase in which very briefly held brooding chords alternate with long-held ones. Then, after a noble chord sequence, on to a phrase in a more fluid rhythm but equally rich and somber harmony: at all events, there's no mistaking that this is the high country. The meditative material of the introductory passage contrasts almost completely with what will follow. Below this a rumbling in the bass heralds the first subject, which literally springs from the depths.

The main subject of this high-strung, combative sonata movement (marked *allegro con brio ed appassionato*, or fast, with brilliance, and impassioned) is a rip-snorting idea that takes a few angry paws at the ground before unfolding in the short-short-long rhythmic figure that dominates its course. The remainder of the theme is a succession of banged-out unisons and raging sixteenth notes that tell us that the fighting Beethoven we know so well is back. But some hesitations in the phrasing and a sorrow-laden ending to the long tune suggest weariness in the old warrior. The second portion of the opening statement involves a *fugato* passage in which sixteenth notes in the right hand battle eighth notes in the left, then switch positions; Beethoven seasons this movement heavily with counterpoint without ever getting a full fugue going. The sequence ends with a variant of the high- and low-note idea as the player crosses the left hand to play high, then low, then high again, over a boiling *tremolando* in the right. The second theme, a strange, operatic passage, is built on a cadenza-like phrase that Beethoven contrives to make at once skittish and dreamy, the latter by building in pauses and slowdowns. But a sequence of crashing sixteenth notes at the original tempo signals a return to battle. This is followed by a playing-out of the short-short-long melody in the bass, now fully developed in militarist garb, unforgettable and terrifying. Another sequence of nerve-rattling sixteenth notes leads to a repeat of the exposition.

The development opens with the short-short-long motto set forth softly in another magnificent *fugato* passage, filled with mystery and a hint of terror. But Beethoven soon breaks this apart, obsessively repeating the motto over rising arpeggios in the left hand; finally, there is a repeat of the main theme in its first incarnation. Some bare octaves hammer the theme in syncopation, leading to another boiling *fugato* passage that throws eighth and sixteenth notes into battle again. The sixteenths win out in a withering, pain-filled passage that ends in the high low hand-crossing sequence. The second theme, which seems to exist in a different world far from that of the battle-scarred first subject, reappears, followed by four beautiful arpeggios over a thoughtful melody in the bass. This is soon swept away by screaming sixteenth notes and the militarist incarnation of the first theme, but an eight-chord sequence cools things down.

The coda, quieter but not lacking in drama, is based on new material, consisting of chords in a rowing rhythm that pull quietly but insistently away from C minor over majestic rumbling sixteenth notes in the left hand. A diminished seventh chord shudders like faraway thunder, and suddenly we end, quietly, in a clouded C major.

The structure of the second movement is relatively straightforward: it's a slow, songful theme in two parts, followed by three strict variations, a fourth that's in double variation form, then a long, fantasia-like coda to end the movement. None of this addresses the utter magic of the music contained in its 177 measures, or the amazing blend of simplicity and complexity it represents, or the distances it seems to travel in the course of its normal playing time of seventeen or eighteen minutes. Here is an incomparable example of the transformative power of music, beginning in one place and time, but leaving the listener someplace far distant and other at its conclusion.

Beethoven titles the movement Arietta, which of course means "little aria," a curious name for this short but heartfelt theme, followed by the tempo indication *Adagio molto semplice e cantabile*: slow, very simply and songfully—indeed. The tempo applies to the entire movement, which seems to get faster, but only because Beethoven keeps using shorter, faster notes as he proceeds. The tempo and pulse never change, giving the movement unity over its great length and downpour of notes.

He sculpts the theme lovingly, as you might expect: the opening phrase falls, as does the second; then the next two arch upward nobly and memorably, completing the first half of the melody. As is common with themes, the second half mirrors the first, but stays closer to the chords of the harmonic underpinning, which are extraordinarily simple (there's Beethoven's *molto semplice*). Beethoven does, however, build in some unmistakable dissonances that occupy a key role as the variations play out. His time signature is a highly unusual 9/16, but don't worry about that when you listen; just try to catch the soulfulness, spirituality, and preternatural calm of the thing. Both halves of the theme are repeated.

The first variation breaks the theme into the gentlest of movements and sweetest of harmonic possibilities. In the second, Beethoven amplifies the sense of motion further by working in faster note values; the feeling of ineffable sweetness persists with melting sixths, and some chords seem to reach at something outside the texture. In the third variation Beethoven uses a sharp rhythm to convey the wildest excitement; textures are thick, and the music has an almost jazzlike feel. In the first half, Beethoven forces the theme to plunge downward almost dizzily from high on the keyboard; in the responding second half, it seems to have to force its way upward from far down.

With the beginning of the fourth variation, the bottom seems to drop out. Soft chords pulse in the right hand, which is set low above a gentle rumbling far below in the left. The theme is embedded in these gentle chords, sounding almost like deep breathing, but it's difficult at first to make out—give yourself time. Suddenly sweet scales rise up, and the repeat of the theme is sung high on the keyboard, its harmony shared between the luxuriant ornamentation of the right hand and the dainty, almost plucked quality of the left. This passage is reminiscent of the last variation of the third movement of Op. 109, where the theme is carried in a flood of little notes; but where that is a torrent, this is a gentler, stranger stream.

Beethoven gives us the second half as he did the first, with the first iteration deep in the keyboard in the beautiful pulsing chords over the distant rumbling quick notes in the bass, followed by the ascent to the high range of the keyboard where it is sung out delicately in high figuration. But tones foreign to the harmony and dreamy, crystalline sonorities creep in, and the listener cannot help but feel the thing is breaking gently apart.

A solemn passage in chords over broad arpeggios sets out the simple harmonic scheme of the theme—C major, A minor, G major, C major—to begin the vast (eighty-one-measure), mystical fantasia-coda. Startling trills break out as Beethoven repeats the falling interval of the theme in new, more remote keys, then stretches the theme in stripped-down form over a perilous four-and-a-half octave gap and near-stillness, where everything seems about to stop. But slowly and hesitantly he pulls back toward the center and into motion, with a passage in C minor between the hands that seems like a celestial dialogue.

A rumbling in the bass heralds the return of the full theme, now sung and danced out ecstatically, over a swift accompaniment of flowing thirty-second notes, and with the dissonances that seemed so soft at first now blazing hotly. The falling interval of the opening melody takes over, then fragments of the theme, played in unmistakable ecstasy that burns out high in the keyboard as the composer, as though seized by a new vision, pulls matters together in a series of trills, then cradles the theme lovingly between a trill high in the right and a gentle rocking in the left, still high on the keyboard—sonorities are crucial here. He also introduces a new harmony to suggest an impending break-up. Soft scales, starting high on the keyboard, work their way sweetly down; the falling fourth of the opening sounds, plainly but sublimely, ending on a calm, soft C major chord, short but unhurried, just below the center of the keyboard.

The Bagatelles and Other Short Pieces

The most famous solo piano work by Beethoven is likely neither the first movement of the "Moonlight" Sonata, or the slow movement of the "Pathétique," but instead the graceful little rondo "Für Elise." The name translates, of course, as "For Elise." Her precise identity, like the date of the work, is not known, although the earliest sketch for the piece in Beethoven's papers is from 1808, marking it as a work of the composer's maturity. "Elise" itself is believed a nickname for one of the composer's *inamorata*, whom the lack of clear dating makes difficult to name.[1] The manuscript was discovered years later among Beethoven's papers, and not published until 1867; its catalog number is WoO 59. Though butchered since then by millions of piano students, it is a work of real merit and charm, not to mention one of the very few by the master that's easy enough for beginners. The questioning figure of its opening phrase seems an immutable part of everyone's internal musical landscape, as are the broad arpeggios that sweep up from beneath to support it. Two episodes consist of a minuet-like passage—the second, a more urgent phrase, with a pulsing accompaniment.

Beethoven described the work on his now-lost manuscript as a "memento," but it's now grouped with the bagatelles, the twenty-four fascinating, mostly short works published as Opp. 33, 119, and 126, in 1803, 1822, and 1824, respectively. The title suggests that the works are trifling in size and significance, but they run the gamut from tiny sketches to elaborate and profound conceptions. The first set of seven (Op. 33) seems to be an assortment that includes at least one very early piece; the rest of the group are harder to date but likely composed circa

1800. Beethoven also assembled the eleven highly varied pieces that make up Op. 119 just before publication from six old ideas and five new. The great Op. 126 was composed in 1824, possibly as recreation from the rigors of the contemporaneous work on the Symphony No. 9. This set of six, more substantial in every way, has longer pieces, which the composer arranged into a suitelike sequence. Op. 126 is, therefore, an important late work, of the greatest interest to pianists and listeners.

Bagatelle, the French word meaning "trifle," emerged as merely one of dozens of titles for keyboard character pieces of the baroque era. The name carries far less substance and structural responsibility than do the nocturne, scherzo, or etude, for instance, let alone the sonata or rondo. It's also a more general rubric, suggesting a short piece, free in form, and rather light in weight. And for the earliest of Beethoven's bagatelles, the title fits. Some of the bagatelles are extremely brief (Nos. 9 and 10 of Op. 119), simply ideas stated once, without flourish. Others, such as Op. 33 No. 4, are set up as a miniature theme and variations. Many are in tripartite (ABA) form, with the opening and closing sections of the same material surrounding a contrasting middle section. The composer assembled Op. 33 from odds and ends to fill a need for marketable short works for publication. In a typically Beethovenian expansion of form, the six of Op. 126 are carefully conceived and sequenced. The musical ideas Beethoven sets out in the bagatelles are pithy, sometimes wild, sometimes almost coarse, and developed in ways that are brief but very well suited to each thought; the form became Beethoven's arena for musings that are profound but always compact.

The Op. 33 set opens with a relaxed miniature rondo, thought to date to the 1780s. But in the abruptly falling scale figures in the first group you'll hear a characteristic capriciousness with a violent undertone that anticipates the mature master's style. The first episode, in A minor key and a floating rhythm, is lovely. The second piece, a scherzo in C major, seems like part of a sonata that never came together. No small piece, it's a fully developed three-part structure, with a swaying minor passage in triplets that recalls and anticipates sections of sonata scherzos from Op. 2 No. 3, Op. 7, and Op. 106. Beethoven's rough playfulness is evident in the closing phrase: eight astonishing bars of syncopated chords interspersed with silences in the keyboard's lower register. It is a daring passage that seems far ahead of its time. Altogether more generic is the third bagatelle, a lilting *allegretto* work in A major that seems modeled on Mozart; it's also cousin to the more developed and interesting second movement of the little Sonata in G Minor, Op. 49 No. 1. What gives it away stylistically as Beethoven's is the thick writing for the left hand in several spots.

With the fourth bagatelle, Beethoven expands his form into a miniature theme and variations. The theme, a sweet and memorable melody in two parts, does indeed beg for the full variation treatment, but all Beethoven gives it is a minor-key incarnation that sways mysteriously up the keyboard, another iteration with the theme deep in the bass, and, a final, ineffable break-up of the melody. The fifth bagatelle combines elements of etude and dance in a sonority and swift pace that are pleasing to hear. It opens with C major arpeggios that race up the keyboard in a waltzlike rhythm, breaking at the top in cascades of sparkling triplets. Beethoven's insistence on aggressive, detached notes at the end of the passage becomes more pronounced over the course of the little work, which is in tripartite form. The middle section, in C minor, mutters in lower registers, in contrast with the outer parts. As he moves the music toward the coda, Beethoven plays more aggressively with the detached notes in a hesitating rhythm, in a manner reminiscent of that of the closing phrase of the second bagatelle of the set.

Beethoven gives to the sixth bagatelle of Op. 33 one of his more interesting combinations of tempo and expressive markings. The tempo, marked *allegretto quasi andante* (moderately quick, as though at a walking pace), covers two adjoining moderate tempi, *allegretto* being slightly faster than *andante*. This is already a pretty fine distinction for the composer to make; but his expression mark, *con un certa espressione parlante*—with a certain speaking expression—is singular and curious. The little D major piece consists of a melody in the right hand that does indeed have a speechlike quality over a left-hand accompaniment that punctuates the thought gently. The touching opening phrase is replied to by a falling one into which a few stronger accents creep. The following section, also dialogue-like, has a more "pathetic" minor-key inflection, but then Beethoven brings back the original ideas, breaking them into flowing sixteenth notes. The composer concludes this unusual two-page musical thought with a coda based on sweetly falling thirds that's fairly long (sixteen measures of a total of eighty-five) for so short a musical paragraph.

Beethoven saves the best in Op. 33 for last (CD Track 3). The *presto* work in A-flat major that ends the series is a wild ride in every way, perhaps throwing light as well into the composer's fast-moving mind and wit. It opens with sharply muttered chords in the left hand, the rhythm firm, fierce, striking. A looping figure beginning at 0:02 swings across in the right hand in a pianistic hook shot; these move so rapidly that they must be repeated just so we can take them in. The arpeggios that sweep harmoniously up and down starting at 0:20 are close cousins to those in the second movement of the Sonata No. 13 in E-flat Major, Op. 27 No. 1. The muttering figure comes back, this time rhythmically amplified by eighth notes (0:41), making it boil vigorously. The looping figure, too, is expanded. More sweet arpeggios shimmer up and down the keyboard (0:57). The muttering returns (1:13), as does the looping theme, and at 1:21 a rising figure pops up in the bass and the right hand is reduced to flying single notes. More furious muttering and looping leads to the opening idea, stated in thick, powerful chords (1:33 and 1:37), and a whiplash dominant proceeding (1:44) to a comically suave closing cadence. No ordinary mind—or nervous system—conceived this astonishing little piece. Note its resemblance to the first movement of the "Waldstein" Sonata (CD Track 4). In the bagatelle, however, the composer deploys his material so wildly that he seems close to losing control, while in the "Waldstein" he uses a very similar idea with more circumspection, as the cornerstone of a big sonata movement—although that, too, has its crazy moments.

The first five of the eleven little works that make up the Op. 119 bagatelles date to an earlier period than 1823, the year of their publication, with some going back to about 1800. The sixth has been dated to 1822.[2] The last five were written as a group in late 1820 and early 1821. Beethoven revised the older pieces thoroughly, assembling the eleven into an artful sequence for publication, so differences in style between the two groups are not particularly marked. The little works do cover a wide range of moods and techniques, as one might expect, and the pieces in Op. 119 include the shortest of all the bagatelles: the entire set has a playing time of about fifteen minutes, compared to around twenty for both Opp. 33 and 126.

An attractive and well-mannered little minuet in G minor opens the set. The opening melody is marked by delicately detached notes, and the tranquil middle section veers into E-flat major. Beethoven breaks the main melody into running notes on its varied return, hinting at deeper, darker emotions. The second bagatelle, in C major, is quirkier in character and features a triplet figure played by the right hand that wiggles above, then crosses below, a steadily rocking accompaniment in the left hand. Soon the wiggling triplet figure lengthens to dominate the texture to the end, which is charmingly unemphatic. "In the Style of a German Dance" is Beethoven's title for the third piece in the set, the exquisite third bagatelle, in D major, of Op. 119. The soaring opening figure is a dazzling sequence, played high on the keyboard. A middle section built of chunky chords over rattling sixteenth notes is the material of the middle section, and of the coda, as well, which is an inspired passage.

The fourth bagatelle of this set is a lyrical sixteen-bar melody of the sort that Beethoven liked to write variations for, a cousin to themes of the Op. 34 set and of the first movement of the Op. 26 sonata. Some unexpected accidentals give the tune a faraway feeling. Beethoven repeats the sequence, embellishing with a few discreet runs and an elegant trill. The fifth bagatelle, in C minor, is a stormy character piece in what a classical-era listener probably perceived as a "riding" rhythm: a thumping beat beneath a nervous melody laden with grace notes, an immense example of which is the opening movement of Haydn's String Quartet in G Minor, Op. 74 No. 3. Contrast and paradox mark the larger, very interesting and funny sixth bagatelle, in G major, which surely began as an improvisation, for the work displays an unusually free construction. It opens calmly with a melodious fragment that is not a fully developed melody. By the fourth bar it pauses on a chord, breaks into a little falling cadenza, then moves smoothly to a series of lightly played chords—all in the first twenty-five seconds. And all has acted as introduction to an innocent, quasi-pastoral tune in a strong 2/4 time signature and short-short-long pattern. Beethoven starts to shake the rhythm into triplets, then into a wilder variation of the tune in dizzy sixteenth notes in 6/8 time. This devolves into a comical passage in which the sixteenth notes play against longer notes; then, in the middle of the bar, Beethoven shifts the time signature back to 2/4, bringing back the innocent theme to end the work almost abruptly, in quiet comedy. What's paradoxical about Op. 119 No. 6 is that it contains seven changes of pattern, takes about ninety seconds to play, yet sounds spacious.

The seventh bagatelle, in C major, is another tiny movement filled with contrasts, moving from a lyrical, trill-laden opening through a passage in a bouncy rhythm and playful spirit and back to the opening idea. A trill starts deep in the bass, and as the harmony thickens, the right hand moves to glittering and grandiose passagework that would not be out of place in Op. 109, for which this almost seems a study in sonority and keyboard layout. The big sonata and little bagatelle are, in fact, contemporaneous. Also in C major, the eighth bagatelle of the set is a small but stately minuet. Dance continues to rule in No. 9, a breathtaking little waltz in A minor on a dashing theme that arches vigorously up the keyboard. Shortest of all these pieces is Op. 119 No. 10, twelve measures long and about twelve seconds' playing time. It's a sweetly breathless study in A major on chords over a syncopated accompaniment. The final bagatelle of Op. 119 is an old-fashioned piece in B-flat major that highlights a beautiful, even melody (Beethoven marks it as "innocent and songful") over a marchlike accompaniment that grows more ethereal as the work progresses. It's a clear inspiration and ancestor of some of the late piano pieces of Brahms.

As noted above, the six bagatelles of Op. 126 are longer, denser, and more substantial in every way than their predecessors. Moreover, Beethoven arranged them carefully into a suite that makes cumulative sense when pieces are played together. Each bagatelle is enriched by the presence of its companions. Beethoven composed the set in early 1824, immediately after finishing the Ninth Symphony; the two works are an astonishing demonstration of his ability to compose on the largest scale and the smallest, though these bagatelles are not miniatures like most of those of Op. 119. Beethoven's last piano works, they are written in his late style: intimate, dense, pithy, and profound, filled with textures and ideas that resemble the final trio of sonatas and the *Diabelli Variations*, and that look forward to the last five string quartets, on which he would soon begin work. First-time listeners should prepare to be bowled over.

The first bagatelle of this set is a lyrical outpouring in G major with a prefatory quality. Its heartfelt melody moves gently but steadily, leading to a central panel that includes a miniature cadenza. Beethoven takes the melodic development high up on the keyboard for the closing section, which sounds like a celestial dialogue. The latter two-thirds of the bagatelle is repeated. The second piece, in G minor, is clearly a companion work. In contrast with the dreamy opening work, it has a wild and rhapsodical tone, from the snap of the opening flourish to the long, dramatic pauses that separate its many iterations. The middle section features a long melody in B-flat major over a pulsing accompaniment. And the beautiful closing passage is part of a long line of sinking, spectral ideas in keyboard works by German composers from Bach to Schumann and Brahms. Beethoven produces another strong contrast with the third bagatelle, in E-flat Major, a magnificent, lyrical outpouring based on a rich melody that seems to expand endlessly, with several grand arpeggios that initiate a variation in the bass beneath a long trill in the right hand. Finally, Beethoven gives the theme back to the right hand in an embroidered form over a more active accompaniment, then breaks it apart one last time, ecstatically, in the brief, quiet, coda.

The fourth bagatelle of Op. 126 is surely one of Beethoven's most remarkable piano works, long or short. This fast, angry piece in modified three-part form is in B minor, a "dark" key that Beethoven regarded warily and never used for another major piece. It opens with a raging theme, almost comic in its truculence, hammered home by furious octaves. This gives way to a more peevish, also rather funny, incarnation of the theme, and a gradual lightening of the tone of the work. Suddenly, the middle part, in B major, breaks in with primitive rising-and-falling scale fragments over a droning bass. This section's remarkable tranquility could not present a more radical contrast with the main theme's barbarous violence. But instead of ending with the fiery opening, Beethoven closes the work with a long page based on the hypnotic middle section. Thus, its form can be shown to be not the three-part ABA, but ABAB.

A profound lyricism pervades the G major fifth bagatelle of Op. 126 from start to finish. This one's in a true tripartite form, opening with a gentle melody in the right hand over an accompaniment in thirds is the left that forms an extension of the melodic strand. In the middle section, the thirds take center stage in a sweetly symmetrical phrase that rises and falls over a steadily flowing left hand. Note, when you listen, to the climactic moment when the melody reaches up to ecstatic chords high in the right hand, far from the left. The sonority of this wide separation is typical of Beethoven's late piano style and can also be heard in the final five sonatas and some of the *Diabelli Variations*, particularly the final one. The opening theme returns, an octave higher, to close this bagatelle tranquilly.

Beethoven builds the final bagatelle, in E-flat major, out of four musical ideas into a remarkable, symmetrical structure. An operatic introductory passage frames the piece—six bustling measures of scales and turns over a *tremolando*-like accompaniment in the left, landing on four dramatic chords. A distinct pause separates the introductory passage from the long, tranquil central panel, which moves at a much slower tempo. This is made up of three distinct ideas, the first of which sounds like a distant horn call; the second is a fervent, complex melodic phrase, and the third is a rising yodeling figure in triplets over a waltz-like left hand. The section continues with a kind of development, in which the yodeling figure is put through some compression and changes of key. Then, at the heart of the piece, the left hand begins a pulsing figure deep in the bass, very much like that of the fourth variation in the second movement of Op. 111, over which the horn call and then the fervent melody are combined and expanded. Not only does the sound resemble Op. 111, but the aesthetic effect is also similar, both works brimming with a faraway ecstasy that belongs only to Beethoven in his late period. The yodeling figure completes the three-part structure of the central section. It also picks up the start of the coda, now in falling triplets, and the horn call comes back, quietly, once more. This great work then ends on a literal repeat of the six-bar opening phrase.

The catalog of Beethoven's works for piano includes more than a few isolated works that are of significance. Several, at least, are worth mentioning. Most unusual is the Fantasia in G Minor, Op. 77, a written-down improvisation of 1809. Fascinating for the view it provides of Beethoven's ability to think on his feet for ten minutes, the piece, like others of its type, is loosely constructed. Mozart's great C Minor Fantasia, K. 475, seems comparable, though more tightly organized. Beethoven begins his with rushing scales, then a gentle melody. Before long, he spins out a more developed, lilting idea, followed by a stormy passage, then a calm-after-the-storm type of theme on which he comes up with a number of variations, ending as he began, on a falling scale. Also interesting is the fantasia's key progression: it begins, of course, in G minor but moves rapidly through a number of tonalities to end in B major. Even at his most daring, this is not something the classicist Beethoven would ordinarily do, but it shows the rapidity of his thought as well as the willingness of his listeners to follow him, like all pianist-composers of the age, wherever he might lead when improvising.

The discarded second movement of the "Waldstein" Sonata (see pp. 81–85), published separately in 1805, is known as the *Andante favori*. It's a long and gracious rondo movement, parts of which have a decidedly old-fashioned feel that would have been completely out of place not only amid the sleek dynamism of Op. 53's outer movements, but displaying others where Beethoven wanders boldly into strange harmonic territory. The composer was right to cut it from the "Waldstein," but the Andante is a work of real merit on its own. Another important one-off is the Rondo a Capriccio in G Major, Op. 129, which carries the nickname "Rage over the Lost Penny" (the title seems to have been, for once, Beethoven's own). This spectacular rondo has been dated to 1823, but some of its material may be older. Supposedly painting a musical picture of a miser looking with ever-growing rage for a lost coin, it stands brilliantly on its own, without a subtitle or program. Beethoven varies the main theme resourcefully, with the episodes acting as witty comple- ments. The tone of the Rondo a Capriccio is undoubtedly humorous, but the composer still puts his material through harmonic changes that are profound.

The Variations

Beethoven published twenty-one independent sets of variations for piano. Most of them are unimportant, four are of great consequence, and a fifth—*Six Variations on an Original Theme*, Op. 76—is light but fun to hear. Based on the familiar rattling "Turkish March" from his incidental music to *The Ruins of Athens*, this brief set is full of charm and the composer's characteristic vigor. Most of the others are formulaic works he composed toward the early part of his career, almost invariably based on themes from long-forgotten operas and ballets of the day, and are never played. The four important sets are the *Six Variations on an Original Theme*, Op. 34, from 1802; *Fifteen Variations and Fugue on an Original Theme*, Op. 35, often referred to as the *"Eroica" Variations*, also from 1802; the Thirty-two Variations in C Minor, WoO 80, composed in 1806; and, preeminently, the *Thirty-three Variations on a Waltz by Diabelli*, Op. 120, of 1819–23.

Beethoven is one of the most important composers to use variation form. As we have seen, he employed it to immense effect in the Sonatas Opp. 26, 57, 109, and 111, as well as in several of the violin sonatas and string quartets, perhaps nowhere more sublimely than in the late quartets, Opp. 127 and 131. The slow movement of the Ninth Symphony is a modified set of variations, too. As we've also seen, he grew to rely more and more on the variation form as he matured, finding it better suited to the more inward nature of his ideas and the more intense, spiritual development they demanded—digging and probing ever deeper into an idea, turning it around, squeezing from it yet another mutation—rather than the inherently conflict-laden sonata form or the more playful rondo.

Variations were popular in Beethoven's age, and he would have heard hundreds of compositions of little worth by minor composers. Haydn and Mozart composed in the genre, and Beethoven would have known Haydn's extraordinary Andante and Variations in F Minor for piano, a masterpiece now less familiar to audiences than its quality merits. Haydn used the variation technique in many other instrumental works as well. Mozart's variations for piano tend toward the lighter side of his works for solo keyboard, which makes them no less enjoyable. The two best-known are probably the twelve charming and elegant *Variations on "Ah, vous dirai-je, Maman,"* K. 265/300e (better known to English-speakers as "Twinkle, Twinkle, Little Star"), while the ten on the tune by Gluck "Unser dummer Pöbel meint," K. 455, are more substantial. Beethoven certainly knew the shattering variation movement that concludes Mozart's Piano Concerto No. 24 in C Minor, K. 491, which helped the younger composer see and scale heights of his own in the variation form.

Bach similarly raised Beethoven's sights, and the relentless power of his passacaglias and chaconnes (a kind of unyielding variation form used by Bach, Handel, and the French keyboard masters of the baroque) inspired his successor's Thirty-two Variations in C Minor. The grandiose scale as well as the immense expressive range of the *Goldberg Variations* served Beethoven as a model for the vast scope and wild comedy of his own *Diabelli Variations*.

The *Six Variations on an Original Theme*, Op. 34, is the sleeper among Beethoven's efforts in the genre, rarely performed in recital or recorded, but of charm, beauty, absolute excellence, and no small daring. The composer pursues several unusual strategies here, chief among which is writing each variation in a different key, a third down from its predecessor, and time signature. Nonmusicians will ask, "So?," but this is a rare if not singular procedure in the variation format, giving the set a more open and free feel than is common in works by Beethoven or any other composer.

The three-part theme is slow, songful, and soulful, not unlike the opening movement of the Op. 26 sonata in character. It's followed by a flowing variation in D major that breaks the theme into rapid passage-work and trills; the second variation, in a springy 6/8 time signature and the key of B-flat major, hops athletically about the keyboard. The third, in G major, moves in tenderly flowing passagework; the fourth is a rather grand minuet in E-flat major. The fifth is a vigorous march in C minor, ending in an unusual fanfare-like passage in C major; and in the sixth, which returns to F major, Beethoven presents the theme in a skipping rhythmic incarnation. But then, in another bold structural move, the composer appends a long coda and a cadenza in which the theme is further dissected and apotheosized, adding what's essentially one more unofficial variation in a remarkable ending to a marvelous work that's as beautiful as it is bold. There aren't many recordings of Op. 34 on the market, but if you look at some of the pianists who've recorded it—Schnabel, Richter, Gould, and Brendel, for instance— you'll make sure to get your hands on a recording, and quickly.

Audiences like the *"Eroica" Variations*, Op. 35. Beethoven used its theme four times in his career, of which the most familiar appearance by far is in the last movement of the Third Symphony—the "Eroica"; hence the nickname. Less often, but more accurately, Op. 35 is called the "Prometheus" Variations, after Beethoven's own ballet score *The Creatures of Prometheus*, Op. 43, of 1800–1801, to reflect the compos- er's first use of the theme. But listeners are always tickled to hear the familiar tune in this less familiar context. This ambitious, generously proportioned work also has a playing time of about twenty-five minutes and is, like most of its contemporary piano pieces by Beethoven, for virtuosos only.

Beethoven opens the set with a fine inspiration. Instead of presenting the full theme directly, he builds it in a complex introductory passage where the theme coalesces from the bottom up. Following a thunder- ous, attention-grabbing E-flat major chord, a quiet statement of the jerky, slightly manic, proto-Stravinskian tune many people think of as the theme but is really just its bass line—its foundation—appears. This contains a fermata that reappears in all fifteen variations, serving as a thematic fingerprint. The composer then adds contrapuntal lines to the bass, first one, then two, then a vigorous three, before present- ing the lilting, pretty theme in its complete incarnation. But we now feel as though we have attended its birth. (Beethoven gives the theme a similar workout at the beginning of the finale of the Third Symphony.)

The first four variations all add some fairly standard types of thematic inversion and ornamentation, from the scurrying triplets of variation 2 to the rapid chord jumps of variation 4, which also anticipates some of the *Diabelli Variations*. With variation 5, however, Beethoven calms the theme down to present it in a more interesting guise of rustic innocence. Variation 6 displays harmonic restlessness as Beethoven shifts tensely between E-flat major to other, related keys, then back again. In the beautiful, moonlit variation 8, Beethoven features hand crossing over steady arpeggios in the first half, followed by swooning harmonies (sixths) in the second. Variation 9, like variation 13 to follow, presents the theme aggressively in hammered grace notes, this one in the bass, and 13 higher up the keyboard.

The interesting tenth variation has a split personality, in which the first part of the theme is set in spotty, pointillist display all over the keyboard, while the second appears in a more menacing legato guise and hammered repeated notes. With variation 11 Beethoven anticipates the comic spirit of the *Diabelli Variations* as the theme comes out in a mincing rhythm, while other comments erupt unexpectedly, and farcically, high and low on the keyboard. Variation 14, a gentle rumination in E-flat minor, sets the stage for the final variation, which is long, in a slow tempo, and as generously decorated as anything Beethoven wrote; it may give an idea of his improvisational style, though of course it's quite polished. A long, expectant coda leads to the fugal finale, another massive passage, which Beethoven finally halts, as though reluctantly, on three big chords. A scale leads to a restatement of the theme in its original, pristine glory; but even here, Beethoven puts it proudly through its paces, making it prance like a thoroughbred amid trills, runs, and triplets. Finally he smoothes the rhythm out for the final passage and closing cadence. But the proportions of the closing section are notable, with the final variation, fugue, and coda occupying nine to ten minutes, or about one-third of the work's total playing time.

A baroque form—the passacaglia—was Beethoven's model for the Thirty-two Variations in C Minor. This type of variation, also called a chaconne, was much favored by the most ambitious musicians of that age, including Purcell, François Couperin, Rameau, J. S. Bach, and Handel. In this form a short (eight-bar) theme, usually stern or majestic, stated in the bass, forms the basis of the whole work; each variation is the same length as the theme, and the form therefore has a relentlessness—sometimes an inflexibility—as the variants keep coming at you. (The playing time of the Thirty-two Variations is all of ten minutes.) It can be a bit much to take, so composers have ways of softening textures or harmony, as Beethoven does here. But the unyielding strictness of the form makes them tough works, and composers have generally used them to express affects from grandeur to much darker feelings. Bach's two famous works in the form, the Chaconne for Solo Violin and the Passacaglia for Organ, stand among that master's darkest instrumental works.

But according to Rosen, Handel's style of passacaglia was Beethoven's model for this work, and the composer was soon unhappy with it, despite its popularity, which continues today.[1] The theme is crisp, strong, and memorable, with the left hand carrying the thematic weight. The first three variations, which are grouped, give a good feel for the character of the piece: in the first, the left hand carries the theme in quick chords, while the right decorates it rapidly; in the second the hands change roles, then variation 3 is all fast notes, with the theme carried within them. To ease the unyielding pace, Beethoven switches to C major for variations 12–16; the flowing, chamber music–like textures of variation 13 resembles the second variation of the second movement of the "Appassionata" more than a little. Variation 17, a beauty, must have inspired Schumann when writing the *Études symphoniques*, his grand essay in the variation form. Beethoven boils the theme to its essential harmonic structure in the quiet variation 23.

And here, too, he packs the end with extra material. Instead of the inevitable eight measures, variation 32 is a generous fifty bars long, containing at least three additional variants as well as some temporizing material—of which there has heretofore been none—in its ample proportions. A final, passionate outburst leads to a quiet close. Beethoven may not have liked the piece, but we may—his standards were higher than ours.

There is nothing quite like the *Thirty-three Variations on a Waltz by Diabelli*, Op. 120—except, of course, for Bach's *Goldberg Variations*.

In this extraordinary work Beethoven takes the plainest material, then transforms it into a masterwork of infinite variety, sophistication, humor, and grandeur, summing up his art and producing what many critics consider his greatest work for piano. Brahms's big variations for piano, the Handel and the Paganini, though splendid and popular, are not in the same league. Its only possible successor is Frederic Rzewski's *36 Variations on "The People United Will Never Be Defeated"* (1975); its one ancestor and undisputed peer is Bach's great and beloved work, which had been published in 1817, but which Beethoven could have known earlier.[2] Readers who have heard Bach's *Goldberg Variations* will sense the kinship between the two enormous sets as they listen to Beethoven's work. That the later master was inspired by the earlier piece seems certain, and one of his goals in composing the *Diabelli* appears to have been the creation of a loving tribute to set alongside the *Goldberg*. Track 9 on the CD that accompanies this book gives the slender theme; tracks 10–18 offer a sampling of Beethoven's astonishing take-offs.

In 1819 the Viennese publisher and occasional composer Anton Diabelli approached Beethoven, as he did dozens of Viennese composers, including Schubert, Mozart's son, and Beethoven's pupil the Archduke Rudolph. Diabelli asked each to write a variation on his bumpy little waltz, which he planned to publish under the title "Patriotic Association of Artists." Beethoven supposedly dismissed the theme as a *Schusterfleck*—a cobbler's patchwork. But before long it had taken hold on his imagination and he had produced nineteen variations.

Beethoven was also at work at this time on a project on the largest scale: the *Missa Solemnis*. So he put the variations aside, resuming them later, and completed them in 1823. By this time, the last piano sonatas had been written, and Beethoven had moved to a new style, in which the musical dramas to be played out were cosmic in scope, and in which the string quartet rather than the piano had begun to dominate the composer's imagination in its final, majestic flight. In any case, Diabelli got way more than he asked for, but he was smart enough to accept Beethoven's massive offering with gratitude and pride, writing in his promotional description that this was "a great and important masterpiece . . . imperishable . . . such a work as only Beethoven, the greatest living representative of true art—only Beethoven and no other, can produce."[3]

Much of the work's humor comes from Beethoven's building so huge a structure on Diabelli's slim foundation. The great English music critic Donald Francis Tovey wrote of Diabelli's theme: "If we look at it from the ordinary point of view, expecting fine sentiments and broad melody, we shall indeed find difficulty in seeing anything in it. The utmost that can be said for it is that it is healthy, unaffected, and drily energetic."[4] Tovey is politely saying that the theme is neutral. Be aware as you get to know the music that the incongruity between the simple theme, track 9 on the CD, and what follows is extreme, and that Diabelli's simplistic harmonic scheme paradoxically frees Beethoven's fertile harmonic imagination, its very neutrality offering him complete latitude in his reinterpretations.

Despite its greatness, however, the *Diabelli* can be one of the more difficult of Beethoven's piano works to appreciate. In it the composer works at the high technical plane typical of his final years, and his comedy is musically sophisticated. A willing listener can learn to "get" some of it, such as the parodies of different eras and composer's styles toward the end, with a little effort; other musical puns are more recondite, though a sense of epic good humor rarely flags. Speaking generally, intellect, lofty musical craft, and Jovian humor rule the *Diabelli Variations*, though of course many moments in it will move you, too. Fortunately, all of the thirty-three have strong profiles and are easy to recall, even on no more than second or third hearings. So give the *Diabelli* time: nothing is better worth your effort. It's also a good piece to follow in score. Please note that the discussion of the variations does not always follow the track sequence on the CD; you'll have to do some jumping about.

Bach arranged the *Goldberg Variations* into groups of three, a procedure Beethoven does not follow. Beethoven's structure for the *Diabelli Variations*, while effective, is not nearly as clear or obvious as Bach's and has long been a source of disagreement. What's certain is that Beethoven's variants move away from the theme as the work progresses, and they do so quickly and decisively: even variations 2 and 3 have already roamed pretty far. In his study on the *Diabelli*, William

Kinderman proposes that the shift from the inward variation 20 to the savage parody of variation 21 marks a turning point in the work.[5] Certainly, few attentive listeners could deny that by then the theme and Beethoven's variations seem almost completely detached; and that the grand variations with which the work concludes (variations 29–33) represent absolute transformations of the humble theme. Kinderman also suggests for a broad structure that the opening variations are variations 1–10, while variations 11–24 form a kind of vast middle section, marked by "dissociation . . . in increasingly radical juxtapositions."[6]

In variations 25–28 Beethoven begins a compressed wind-up toward the crucial final group. The clearest structural element to attend to the first few times you listen to the *Diabelli Variations* is how Beethoven gathers the longest, most earnest variations toward the end. Three in C minor (variations 29, 30, and 31), all in moderate or slow tempo, act as a slow movement, cooling down and adding lyrical spaciousness to what's otherwise a pretty wild, fast-moving work. In this, Beethoven copies Bach, who made variation 25 of the *Goldberg* set long, slow, and tragic, completely different from its companions; Beethoven's variation 31 is a direct tribute to Bach's variation 25. Consider, when you listen to the lavishly ornamented, impassioned lyricism of the *Diabelli* variation 31 (CD Track 16), how far Beethoven has brought the theme, how he has ennobled it and made it expressive beyond any potential you imagined.

The C minor group is followed by variation 32 (CD Track 17), a triumphant double fugue in hammered repeated notes in direct imitation of Handel's contrapuntal manner. This is larger in scale than any variation except for the one that immediately preceded it and, again, a stupendous hyperdevelopment of the little theme. And in Beethoven's erudite joke, the final variation (CD Track 18) is a divine minuet in the high-classical manner of Haydn, Mozart, and, indeed, himself. Its delicacy is at once the apotheosis and the reproach of Diabelli's coarse waltz. Thus, the cycle that begins with that rough little waltz finds consummation, in comic paradox, with the most refined, elegant dance of the previous age.

In spite of the group of serious minor-key variations near the end, comedy plays a crucial role in this grand set. In the funny and memorable variation 9 (CD Track 10) Beethoven presents a pungent, heavy-footed exercise in C minor, filled with obsessively repeated grace notes, shifting harmonies, and emphatic chords, yet sometimes backing off with comic daintiness. This ninth variation is followed by a skittery virtuoso etude that could not be more different in character but is equally comical. Among the variants that seem unarguably comical, foremost is the grotesque variation 13 (CD Track 11), in which Beethoven reduces the theme to a series of thundering, imperious chords alternating with long silences in rhythm, then tiny peeps, filling the harmony in later with chords in crescendo. Variation 1 is a pompous march, comical in that pomposity and standing in closest proximity to the theme. Beethoven found the tune of the opening number of Mozart's opera *Don Giovanni* ("Notte e giorno faticar") in variation 22, another inside joke that tickles knowledgeable listeners (CD Track 14). It also follows Bach's tradition in the *Goldberg Variations*: that master ran two popular songs into the final variation of that work. Kinderman points out that the busy notiness of variation 23 contains a satirical reference to a familiar piano etude by Johann Baptist Cramer—perhaps also a tribute, for Beethoven admired Cramer's playing.[7] Variation 25 (CD Track 15) is a burbling *ländler* in which Beethoven has thrown the harmony and rhythm slightly off. Comedy seems to inhabit many of the thirty-three variations, from the broad satire of the opening variation to the sophisticated musical pun and sublime music of the final minuet.

Variations 16 and 17 are aggressive, closely paired takes on the theme, the first with a trill in the right and broken figuration in the left hand, and the second with the theme pounded out in the left beneath broken figuration, now in the right hand. Other mutations that seem violent are variation 21, which has a dual character alternating seething fury with long, lyrical lines; variation 23; and variation 28, the last before, and contrasting with, the big C minor group.

Among more lyrical incarnations are variation 2, a poetic episode in which Beethoven makes the theme sound wonderfully smooth even while breaking it evenly between the hands; the beautiful *fughetta* (little fugue) that is variation 24; and the triplets of variation 26 that sweep gracefully across the keyboard. A proto-Brahmsian richness pervades the waltz that is variation 8. Of course the C minor variations—29, 30, and 31—are all profoundly lyrical, but these stand apart, forming their own world of introspection and grief. Variation 33, the extraordinary closing minuet, is also deeply expressive.

A fair number of variations, mostly those in which Beethoven plays with the upbeat—the little turn at the beginning of the theme—have an ingratiating charm. These include variations 3, 4, and 8. Variation 11, the coyest of all, practically bats its eyes, and its partner and successor, variation 12, which also makes some astonishing harmonic excursions, falls into this category as well. Although not among these charmingly appealing incarnations, variation 6 is notable for the impressive trill Beethoven makes of the upbeat.

One variation that stands apart for its slow tempo and more solemn posture is variation 14, which moves at a stately, billowing pace, like a distant echo of the rhythms of the French overture in the *Goldberg Variations*. The keyboard textures of variation 18 (CD Track 12) are smooth, but its perpetually shifting harmonies bold. The most forward looking in the entire set is variation 20 (CD Track 13), a series of slow chords that sound as though they had been composed by Debussy or even Bartók, yet the theme is still recognizable through the compressed harmony and distorted rhythms. These thirty-two profound measures show the remarkably advanced state of Beethoven's musical thinking.

As with all abstract music, we're not supposed to draw extramusical associations or conclusions from the *Diabelli Variations*. But Beethoven, as he so often does, makes that task difficult. It's one thing to say someone can "make something from nothing"—but this? Bach's noble theme for the *Goldberg Variations* is his own. Beethoven not only conjures a galaxy of wit from Diabelli's witless waltz, he performs alchemy, turning musical tin into pure gold. Surely one lesson we can take from the *Diabelli Variations* is of the transformative nature of great art.

Beethoven the Companion

The piano was Beethoven's own instrument. He improvised on the piano, seeking inspiration, and worked at the instrument through the compositional processes that followed. And by all accounts Beethoven's own playing was some of the greatest of the age, and probably the most moving. Biographers and critics have come to the conclusion that his works for the keyboard run ahead of others stylistically—that they are the works where he tried out new styles before expanding his concepts to other forms. Thus, for example, he conceived the advanced ideas and expression of the Piano Sonatas Opp. 26, 27, and 28 in 1801, and the more conservative string quartets of Op. 18 in 1799 and 1800. The Symphony No. 2, completed in 1802, may be a big and exciting example of its species, but it is, nevertheless, a symphony in the high-classical style of Haydn. Later in Beethoven's career, it's the "Hammerklavier" Sonata that initiates the late period so forcefully. More examples might be cited. There's a certain sense to this: it must have been easier for the composer to experiment in works he could play himself, testing ideas without having to teach or explain them to other musicians.

The listener who makes his or her way more or less chronologically through the music for solo piano may find that they seem rather more intimate and personal than those in other genres for larger ensembles. (The piano concertos, being display pieces, don't fit this characterization as well.) Thus, it may be that it is through the sonatas, the bagatelles, and those few crucial sets of variations that Beethoven reveals himself to us most clearly. Certainly some of the thirty-two sonatas— the "Pathétique," the "Appassionata," and the "Hammerklavier"—are "public" works, meant to impress in live performance. But many, too, are intimate and reflective, each with its distinct character, from the two little gems of Op. 14 to the great two-movement sonatas, Opp. 54, 78, and 90 and, consummately, the remarkable Op. 101. And think of the many-faceted humor of the *Diabelli Variations*, in which rough musical jokes jostle with the most refined and sophisticated musical technique. Or remember the fury and grandeur of the "Appassionata," in which Beethoven lays out a tragic vision in abstract music. Remember, too, the luxuriant fantasy of Op. 109, the suffering and joy expressed in Op. 110—and the sweet nature and confessional quality of both works. And consider the struggle and otherworldly remove of Op. 111's two movements.

It may be not going too far to suggest that the works for solo piano, more than any other part of Beethoven's oeuvre, come closest to being the composer's personal diary. Through them, more than through the grandly ambitious symphonies or the intellectually rigorous string quartets, we come to know the spirit of the man, so that he becomes our sublime and brilliant companion.

The consumer who wants to listen to Beethoven's piano music faces the happy problem of an excess supply of worthwhile recordings by fine pianists. A look at the Arkivmusic Web site reveals dozens of performances of the least-recorded sonatas and almost 250 of the most popular—the "Appassionata." There are about a dozen recordings of the complete thirty-two, including fine ones by revered old-timers including Artur Schnabel, Wilhelm Backhaus, Wilhelm Kempff, and Annie Fischer, as well as others by living masters, including Alfred Brendel, Vladimir Ashkenazy, Daniel Barenboim, and Richard Goode. The story is the same for the concertos. This situation almost always makes it impossible to recommend specific artists or recordings. To mention one is to overlook ten, and I have only heard a fraction of the performances out there. Recordings mentioned in the text are generally included to illustrate or to make a specific point.

That said, those that this longtime listener likes are Schnabel's landmark recordings from the 1930s; though the sound is rough and mistakes plentiful, Schnabel's technique and dashing style, which somehow summons profundity whenever called for, remain unbeatable. Among modern performers, Goode's warmhearted and poetic complete recording from the mid-1990s is a personal favorite. The performances of eighteen of the sonatas and the five concertos recorded by the great British pianist Solomon in the 1950s are of a sublime austerity and ought not to be missed. Ivan Moravec's performances of six sonatas, the Thirty-two Variations in C Minor, and the Fourth Piano Concerto make one wish he would record more Beethoven, and at least some of the many recordings of the sonatas by Sviatoslav Richter are brilliant, as are the great Russian's performances of the Opp. 34 and 35 variations as well as the *Diabelli*. Stephen Kovacevich's recording of the *Diabelli Variations* is worth looking for. Krystian Zimerman's performances of the concertos with the Vienna Philharmonic under Leonard Bernstein are a bit slow in tempo, but very satisfying. Again, please remember that these are only some favorites among the recordings I know, and that there are surely many other fine performances that I haven't heard.

Notes

Chapter 1

1. Schonberg, 81.
2. Ibid., 94–95.
3. Lockwood, 289.
4. Rosen, *Beethoven's Piano Sonatas*, 117–20.
5. Tovey, *The Forms of Music*, 200.
6. Rosen, *The Classical Style*, 438.

Chapter 2

1. Two of the best recent studies of Beethoven's life and complete oeuvre are Lockwood, *Beethoven: The Music and the Life*, and Cooper, *Beethoven*; see the bibliography for details.
2. Quoted in Lockwood, 47.
3. Quoted in ibid., 50.
4. Cooper, *Beethoven*, 52–53.
5. Lockwood, 196.
6. Ibid., 300–301.
7. Ibid., p. 233.
8. Cf. Cooper, *Beethoven*, 376.
9. von Breuning, 44.
10. Quoted in Lockwood, 197.
11. Cooper, *Beethoven*, 153–54, 247, and 333.
12. von Breuning, 72.

Chapter 3

1. Plantinga, 3–6.
2. Quoted in Cooper, *Beethoven*, 110.
3. Plantinga, 7.
4. Ibid., 109.
5. Ibid., 113–35 and 150–58.
6. Ibid., 141.

Chapter 4

1. Plantinga, 211.
2. Ibid., 255.
3. Ibid., 360.

Chapter 5

1. Rosen, *Beethoven's Piano Sonatas*, 129.
2. Tovey, *A Companion to Beethoven's Pianoforte Sonatas*, 50.
3. Liner notes, Beethoven, *Piano Sonatas: Moonlight—Pathétique—The Tempest—Appassionata*, Maria João Pires, piano (Apex CD 8573892252, 2001).

Chapter 6

1. Cooper, *Beethoven*, 92.
2. Tovey, *A Companion to Beethoven's Pianoforte Sonatas*, 82.
3. Page, 459.
4. Tovey, *A Companion to Beethoven's Pianoforte Sonatas*, 90.
5. Anatole Leikin, "The Sonatas," in Samson, *The Cambridge Companion to Chopin*, 161.
6. Tovey, *A Companion to Beethoven's Pianoforte Sonatas*, 100–103.
7. Ibid., 104.

Chapter 7

1. Rosen, *Beethoven's Piano Sonatas*, 164.
2. "WoO" stands for "Werke ohne Opus," or works without opus number.
3. Tovey, *A Companion to Beethoven's Pianoforte Sonatas*, 149–50.

Chapter 8

1. Lockwood, 299.
2. Rosen, *Beethoven's Piano Sonatas*, 197.
3. Tovey, *A Companion to Beethoven's Pianoforte Sonatas*, 180.
4. Rosen, *Beethoven's Piano Sonatas*, 205.
5. Cooper, *Beethoven*, 272.

Chapter 9

1. Quoted in Rosen, *Beethoven's Piano Sonatas*, 228.
2. Quoted in Cooper, *Beethoven*, 281.
3. Friskin and Freundlich, 89.
4. Tovey, *A Companion to Beethoven's Pianoforte Sonatas*, 220.

Chapter 10

1. Schonberg, 249.
2. Ibid., 275.
3. Rosen, *The Classical Style*, 67–68.

Chapter 11

1. Cooper, *Beethoven*, 208–9.
2. Alfred Brendel, preface to Beethoven, *Bagatelles*, iv.

Chapter 12

1. Rosen, *The Classical Style*, 400–401.
2. Lockwood, 394.
3. Quoted in Tovey, *Chamber Music*, 124.
4. Ibid., 125.
5. Kinderman, 103–4.
6. Ibid., 110.
7. Ibid., 104–6.

Selected Bibliography

Beethoven, Ludwig van. *Bagatelles*. Preface by Alfred Brendel. Vienna: Wiener Urtext, Schott/Universal Edition, 1968.

————. *Complete Variations for Solo Piano from the Breitkopf & Härtel Edition*. Mineola, NY: Dover, 1986.

————. *Complete Pianoforte Sonatas*. Edited by Harold Craxton. Annotated by Donald Francis Tovey. 3 vols. London: Associated Board of the Royal Schools of Music, 1932.

————. *Complete Piano Sonatas*. Edited by Artur Schnabel. 2 vols. Melville, NY: Belwin Mills by arrangement with Edizioni Curci, Milano, 1949.

————. *Klavierkonzert No. 1*. Study score. Edited by Hans-Werner Küthen. Munich: G. Henle, 1984.

————. *Klavierkonzert No. 2*. Study score. Edited by Hans-Werner Küthen. Munich: G. Henle, 1984.

————. *Klavierkonzert No. 3*. Study score. Edited by Hans-Werner Küthen. Munich: G. Henle, 1990.

————. *Klavierkonzert No. 4*. Study score. Edited by Hans-Werner Küthen. Munich: G. Henle, 1990.

————. *Piano Concerto No. 5*. Study score. Edited by Wilhelm Altmann. London: Ernst Eulenberg, 1933.

Cooper, Barry. *Beethoven*. Oxford: Oxford University Press, 2008.

————. *Beethoven and the Creative Process*. Oxford: Clarendon, 1992.

Dahlhaus, Carl. *Nineteenth Century Music*. Translated by J. Bradford Robinson. Berkeley: University of California Press, 1989.

Friskin, James, and Irwin Freundlich. *Music for the Piano*. New York: Dover, 1973.

Kennedy, Michael, ed. *The Oxford Dictionary of Music*. 2nd ed. Oxford: Oxford University Press, 1994.

Kinderman, William. *Beethoven's "Diabelli Variations": Studies in Musical Genesis and Structure*. Oxford: Oxford University Press, 1989.

Lockwood, Lewis. *Beethoven: The Music and the Life*. New York: W. W. Norton, 2003.

Page, Tim, ed. *The Glenn Gould Reader*. New York: Alfred A. Knopf, 1984.

Plantinga, Leon. *Beethoven's Concertos: History, Style, Performance*. New York: W. W. Norton, 1999.

Rosen, Charles. *Beethoven's Piano Sonatas: A Short Companion*. New Haven, CT: Yale University Press, 2002.

————. *The Classical Style: Haydn, Mozart, Beethoven*. New York: W. W. Norton, 1972.

Samson, Jim, ed. *The Cambridge Companion to Chopin*. Cambridge: Cambridge University Press, 1992.

Schonberg, Harold C. *The Great Pianists*. New York: Fireside Books, 1987.

Sullivan, J. W. N. *Beethoven: His Spiritual Development*. New York: Vintage Books, 1960.

Tovey, Donald Francis. *Chamber Music*. Oxford: Oxford University Press, 1989.

————. *The Forms of Music*. New York: World, 1972.

————. *A Companion to Beethoven's Pianoforte Sonatas: A Bar-by-Bar Analysis*. London: Associated Board of the Royal Schools of Music, 1931.

von Breuning, Gerhard. *Memories of Beethoven*. Edited by Maynard Solomon. Translated by Henry Mins and Maynard Solomon. Cambridge: Cambridge University Press, 1992.

CD Track Listing

1. Piano Concerto No. 2 in B-flat Major, Op. 19: Rondo:
   Molto allegro (6:32)
   Idil Biret, piano; the Bilkent Symphony Orchestra, conducted by Antoni Wit
   From Naxos CD 8.571253

2. Sonata No. 1 in F Minor, Op. 2 No. 1: Prestissimo
   (fourth movement) (5:01)
   Jenö Jandó, piano
   From Naxos CD 8.550150

3. Bagatelle in A-flat Major, Op. 33 No. 7 (1:57)
   Jenö Jandó, piano
   From Naxos CD 8.550474

4. Sonata No. 21 in C Major, Op. 53 "Waldstein": Allegro con brio
   (10:29)
   Jenö Jandó, piano
   From Naxos CD 8.550054

5. Sonata No. 21 in C Major, Op. 53 "Waldstein": Introduzione:
   Molto adagio; Rondo: Allegretto moderato (12:59)
   Jenö Jandó, piano
   From Naxos CD 8.550054

6. Sonata No. 31 in A-flat Major, Op. 110: Moderato cantabile,
   molto espressivo (6:21)
   Jenö Jandó, piano
   From Naxos CD 8.550151

7. Sonata No. 31 in A-flat Major, Op. 110: Allegro molto (2:20)
Jenö Jandó, piano
From Naxos CD 8.550151

8. Sonata No. 31 in A-flat Major, Op. 110: Adagio, ma non
troppo—Fuga: Allegro, ma non troppo (10:42)
Jenö Jandó, piano
From Naxos CD 8.550151

9. *Diabelli Variations*, Op. 120: Theme, by Anton Diabelli (0:53)
Edmund Battersby, piano
From Naxos CD 8.557385

10. *Diabelli Variations*, Op. 120: Variation 9: Allegro pesante
e risoluto (1:39)
Edmund Battersby, piano
From Naxos CD 8.557385

11. *Diabelli Variations*, Op. 120: Variation 13: Vivace (1:08)
Edmund Battersby, piano
From Naxos CD 8.557385

12. *Diabelli Variations*, Op. 120: Variation 18: Poco moderato (1:32)
Edmund Battersby, piano
From Naxos CD 8.557385

13. *Diabelli Variations*, Op. 120: Variation 20: Andante (2:15)
Edmund Battersby, piano
From Naxos CD 8.557385

14. *Diabelli Variations*, Op. 120: Variation 22: Allegro molto alla
"Notte e giorno faticar" di Mozart (0:52)
Edmund Battersby, piano
From Naxos CD 8.557385

15. *Diabelli Variations*, Op. 120: Variation 25: Allegro (0:53)
Edmund Battersby, piano
From Naxos CD 8.557385

16. *Diabelli Variations*, Op. 120: Variation 31: Largo, molto
espressivo (4:14)
Edmund Battersby, piano
From Naxos CD 8.557385

17. *Diabelli Variations*, Op. 120: Variation 32: Fuga—Allegro (3:14)
Edmund Battersby, piano
From Naxos CD 8.557385

18. *Diabelli Variations*, Op. 120: Variation 33: Tempo di menuetto,
moderato (4:01)
Edmund Battersby, piano
From Naxos CD 8.557385

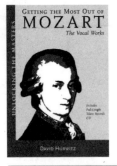

UNLOCKING THE MASTERS

The highly acclaimed Unlocking the Masters series brings readers into the world of the greatest composers and their music. All books come with CDs that have tracks taken from the world's foremost libraries of recorded classics, bringing the music to life.

"With infectious enthusiasm and keen insight, the Unlocking the Masters series succeeds in opening our eyes, ears, hearts, and minds to the great composers." – *Strings*

**BACH'S CHORAL MUSIC:
A LISTENER'S GUIDE**
by Gordon Jones
$22.99 • 978-1-57467-180-3
HL00332767

**BACH'S KEYBOARD MUSIC:
A LISTENER'S GUIDE**
by Victor Lederer
$22.99 • 978-1-57467-182-7
HL00332830

**BEETHOVEN'S PIANO MUSIC:
A LISTENER'S GUIDE**
by Victor Lederer
$22.99 • 978-1-57467-194-0
HL00333060

**BEETHOVEN'S SYMPHONIES:
A GUIDED TOUR**
by John Bell Young
$22.99 • 978-1-57467-169-8
HL00331951

**BERNSTEIN'S ORCHESTRAL MUSIC:
AN OWNER'S MANUAL**
by David Hurwitz
$24.99 • 978-1-57467-193-3
HL00332912

BRAHMS: A LISTENER'S GUIDE
by John Bell Young
$22.99 • 978-1-57467-171-1
HL00331974

**CHOPIN: A LISTENER'S GUIDE
TO THE MASTER OF THE PIANO**
by Victor Lederer
$22.95 • 978-1-57467-148-3
HL00331699

**DEBUSSY:
THE QUIET REVOLUTIONARY**
by Victor Lederer
$22.95 • 978-1-57467-153-7
HL00331743

**DVOŘÁK: ROMANTIC MUSIC'S
MOST VERSATILE GENIUS**
by David Hurwitz
$27.95 • 978-1-57467-107-0
HL00331662

THE GREAT INSTRUMENTAL WORKS
by M. Owen Lee
$27.95 • 978-1-57467-117-9
HL00331672

**EXPLORING HAYDN:
A LISTENER'S GUIDE TO
MUSIC'S BOLDEST INNOVATOR**
by David Hurwitz
$27.95 • 978-1-57467-116-2
HL00331671

LISZT: A LISTENER'S GUIDE
by John Bell Young
$22.99 • 978-1-57467-170-4
HL00331952

**THE MAHLER SYMPHONIES:
AN OWNER'S MANUAL**
by David Hurwitz
$22.99 • 978-1-57467-099-8
HL00331650

**OPERA'S FIRST MASTER:
THE MUSICAL DRAMAS OF
CLAUDIO MONTEVERDI**
by Mark Ringer
$29.95 • 978-1-57467-110-0
HL00331665

**GETTING THE MOST OUT OF
MOZART:
THE INSTRUMENTAL WORKS**
by David Hurwitz
$22.95 • 978-1-57467-096-7
HL00331648

**GETTING THE MOST OUT OF
MOZART: THE VOCAL WORKS**
by David Hurwitz
$22.95 • 978-1-57467-106-3
HL00331661

**PUCCINI:
A LISTENER'S GUIDE**
by John Bell Young
$22.95 • 978-1-57467-172-8
HL00331975

**SCHUBERT: A SURVEY OF HIS
SYMPHONIC, PIANO, AND
CHAMBER MUSIC**
by John Bell Young
$22.99 • 978-1-57467-177-3
HL00332766

**SCHUBERT'S THEATER OF SONG:
A LISTENER'S GUIDE**
by Mark Ringer
$22.99 • 978-1-57467-176-6
HL00331973

**SHOSTAKOVICH SYMPHONIES
AND CONCERTOS:
AN OWNER'S MANUAL**
by David Hurwitz
$22.99 • 978-1-57467-131-5
HL00331692

**SIBELIUS, THE ORCHESTRAL
WORKS: AN OWNER'S MANUAL**
by David Hurwitz
$27.95 • 978-1-57467-149-0
HL00331735

**TCHAIKOVSKY:
A LISTENER'S GUIDE**
by Daniel Felsenfeld
$27.95 • 978-1-57467-134-6
HL00331697

**DECODING WAGNER:
AN INVITATION TO HIS WORLD
OF MUSIC DRAMA**
by Thomas May
$27.99 • 978-1-57467-097-4
HL00331649

AMADEUS PRESS

www.amadeuspress.com